No-Guilt Desserts

Over 120 Recipes
200 Calories or Less!

PUBLICATIONS INTERNATIONAL, LTD.

Front cover photo and photo on page 32 by Kathy Sanders, Chicago, Illinois.

Pictured on the front cover (*clockwise from top*): Tropical Bar Cookie (*page 35*), Mini Almond Cheesecake (*page 9*), Chocolate Chip Cookie (*page 33*), Creamy Frozen Yogurt (*page 68*) and Chocolate Orange Delight (*page 21*).

Pictured on the back cover (*from top to bottom*): Nutty Blueberry Muffins (*page 47*), Pear Bistro Tart (*page 31*), Apricot Frappé and Strawberry Frosty (*page 90*) and Lemon Ginger Sauce (*page 87*).

ISBN 0-7853-0069-4

This edition published by:
Publications International, Ltd.
7373 N. Cicero Avenue
Lincolnwood, IL 60646

Printed and bound in U.S.A.

9   8   7   6   5   4   3   2   1

Microwave ovens vary in wattage and power output; cooking times given with microwave directions in this book may need to be adjusted.

No-Guilt Desserts

Sweet

◆◆◆

TEMPTATIONS

You Can Have Your Cake and Eat It, Too!

Like many people today, you're probably concerned about the way you eat. You'd like to make better choices about the foods you prepare, to cut down on calories, fat, cholesterol and sodium, but you also love to eat—especially dessert. Now there's a collection of recipes that will let you indulge in dessert *without* indulging in all the calories. With over 170 recipes from America's top food companies, NO-GUILT DESSERTS offers you a wide variety of dessert choices—from sinlessly rich cakes and cheesecakes, scrumptious cookies, sure-fire snacks, light ice creams and frozen yogurts, luscious pies, enticing breads, muffins and coffeecakes, fabulous fruit desserts and much much more—all of them lower in calories and fat than you would expect.

Making Smart Choices

The American Heart Association has offered guidelines to help people adjust their diets to try to prevent heart and vascular diseases and we've followed those guidelines in choosing recipes for this book. The recipes that follow can help you make smart, healthy decisions about the desserts you prepare. Every recipe in this book is followed by a nutritional chart that tells you the number of calories, the grams (g) of fat, the milligrams (mg) of sodium and the milligrams of cholesterol for each serving of that recipe. To be considered for this book, recipes had to contain 300 calories or less per serving, and contain no more than 10 grams of fat per serving. As an

extra bonus, most of the desserts offered here are less than 200 calories per serving and many are even under 100 calories per serving.

Many of the recipes are low-sodium and low-cholesterol as well. These recipes contain less than 300 mg of sodium and less than 50 mg of cholesterol per serving. As you browse through the book you'll see that most of the recipes fall well below these numbers. You can easily find these recipes by looking for the color bars below each recipe title:

Under 200 Calories

Under 100 Calories

Low Sodium

Low Cholesterol

The values of 300 calories, 10 g of fat, 300 mg sodium and 50 mg cholesterol per serving, were chosen after careful consideration of a number of factors. The Food and Nutrition Board of the National Academy of Sciences proposes the Recommended Dietary Allowances (RDAs) for all nutritive components including calories, carbohydrates, fat, protein, amino acids, vitamins and minerals. The RDAs were most recently revised in 1989. The RDA for calories is broken down according to age groups and sex. For men between the ages of 19 and 50, for example, the RDA for total calorie intake is 2,900 calories per day. For women between the ages of 19 and 50, it is 2,200 calories per day. Thus, the 300 calories or less per serving for the recipes in this book represents only about 10 percent of the RDA for most men and about 14 percent of the RDA for most women.

The American Heart Association has recommended that total fat intake should be less than 30 percent of calories. For most women that amounts to about 660 calories from fat (or about 73 grams of fat) per day; for most men about 870 calories or about 97 grams of fat per day. Thus the 10 grams of fat or less per serving for each recipe in this book represents a reasonable amount for a single dessert in a single meal. The American Heart Association also recommends that sodium intake not exceed 3,000 mg a day, and cholesterol intake be less than 300 mg a day. The numbers we chose for recipes to be considered low-sodium (300 mg or less) or low-cholesterol (50 mg or less) are also well within these guidelines.

About the Nutritional Information

The analysis of each recipe includes all the ingredients that are listed in that recipe, except ingredients labeled as "optional" or "for garnish." If a range is given in the yield of a recipe ("Makes 6 to 8 servings," for example), the *higher* yield was used to calculate the per serving information. If a range is offered for an ingredient ("¼ to ⅛ teaspoon," for example) the *first* amount given was used to calculate the nutrition information. If an ingredient is presented with an option ("2 tablespoons margarine or butter," for example) the *first* item listed was used to calculate the nutrition information. Foods shown in photographs on the same serving plate or offered as "serve with" suggestions at the end of a recipe are *not* included in the recipe analysis unless stated in the per serving line.

The nutrition information that appears with each recipe was submitted by the participating companies and associations. **Every effort has been made to check the accuracy of these numbers. However, because numerous variables account for a wide range of values for certain foods, all nutritive analyses that appear in this book should be considered approximate.** For consistency, many of the figures in the nutrition charts have been rounded to the nearest whole number. The figures in the nutrition charts are based on the nutritive values for foods in the U.S. Department of Agriculture Composition of Foods Handbook No. 8 (series), or from values submitted directly by the food manufacturers themselves. (For more information, see the introductions to the Handbook No. 8 series.)

What This Book Does and Does Not Do

The recipes in this book were all selected to help you make smart choices about the desserts you want to enjoy. And with more than 170 recipes contributed by America's largest food companies, you'll find plenty to choose from. From elegant cakes to serve to guests, to quick and easy cookies for kids, you're sure to find low-calorie, low-fat desserts for almost any occasion.

This book offers you a wide variety of recipes that are, on a per serving basis, lower in calories, fat, cholesterol and sodium than regular desserts. **The recipes in this book are NOT intended as a medically therapeutic program, nor as a substitute for medically approved diet plans for people on cholesterol-, fat- or sodium-restricted diets. You should consult your physician before beginning any diet plan.** The recipes offered here can be part of a healthy lifestyle that meets recognized dietary guidelines. A healthy lifestyle includes not only eating a balanced diet, but engaging in appropriate exercise as well.

By preparing desserts that are low in calories, fat, cholesterol and sodium, you can actually enjoy your favorite part of the meal. And with the wonderful variety offered here, you don't have to sacrifice either flavor or convenience. So let yourself go and give in to guilt-free sweet indulgence!

Della Robbia Cake

Light & Luscious
CAKES

Della Robbia Cake

> **Under 200 Calories**

Makes 12 servings

Cake
- 1 package DUNCAN HINES® Angel Food Cake Mix
- 1½ teaspoons grated lemon peel

Glaze
- 6 tablespoons sugar
- 1½ tablespoons cornstarch
- 1 cup water
- 1 tablespoon lemon juice
- ½ teaspoon vanilla extract
  Few drops red food coloring
- 6 cling peach slices
- 6 medium strawberries, sliced

1. Preheat oven to 375°F.

2. **For Cake**, prepare following package directions adding lemon peel with Cake Flour Mixture (red "B" packet). Bake and cool following package directions.

3. **For Glaze**, combine sugar, cornstarch and water in small saucepan. Cook over medium-high heat until mixture thickens and is clear. Remove from heat. Stir in lemon juice, vanilla extract and red food coloring.

4. Alternate peach slices with strawberry slices around top of cooled cake. Pour glaze over fruit and top of cake. Refrigerate leftovers.

Nutrients per serving:			
Calories	145	Sodium	100 mg
Fat	0 g	Cholesterol	0 mg

Chocolate Cake Fingers

> **Under 100 Calories**

Makes 30 servings

- 1 cup granulated sugar
- 1 cup all-purpose flour
- ⅓ cup HERSHEY'S® Cocoa
- ¾ teaspoon baking powder
- ¾ teaspoon baking soda
- ½ cup skim milk
- ¼ cup frozen egg substitute, thawed
- ¼ cup canola or vegetable oil
- 1 teaspoon vanilla extract
- ½ cup boiling water
  Powdered sugar
- 1 teaspoon freshly grated orange peel
- 1½ cups frozen non-dairy whipped topping, thawed
- 30 fresh strawberries or raspberries (optional)

Heat oven to 350°F. Line bottom of 13×9×2-inch baking pan with wax paper. In large mixer bowl, stir together sugar, flour, cocoa, baking powder and baking soda. Add milk, egg substitute, oil and vanilla; beat on medium speed of electric mixer 2 minutes. Add water; stir with spoon until well blended. Pour batter into prepared pan. Bake 16 to 18 minutes or until wooden pick inserted in center comes out clean. Place clean towel on wire rack; sprinkle with powdered sugar. Invert cake onto towel; peel off wax paper. Turn cake right side up onto wire rack. Cool completely. Cut cake into small rectangles (about 2¼×1¼ inches). Stir orange peel into whipped topping; spoon dollop on each piece of cake. Garnish each serving with strawberry or raspberry, if desired.

Nutrients per serving:			
Calories	80	Sodium	35 mg
Fat	3 g	Cholesterol	0 mg

Raspberry Shortcake

Under 200 Calories

Makes 8 servings

1½ cups whole frozen raspberries, divided
4½ tablespoons sugar, divided
  1 cup all-purpose flour
  1 teaspoon baking powder
  ¼ teaspoon baking soda
  1 tablespoon margarine
  1 egg white
  ⅓ cup evaporated skim milk
  ¼ teaspoon almond extract
  ¾ cup low-fat cottage cheese
1½ teaspoons sugar
  1 teaspoon lemon juice

Preheat oven to 450°F. Spray baking sheet with non-stick cooking spray. In small bowl, toss 1¼ cups of the raspberries with 2½ tablespoons sugar; refrigerate. In medium bowl, stir together flour, baking powder, baking soda and remaining 2 tablespoons sugar. Cut in margarine using pastry blender or 2 knives. In separate bowl, beat egg white, evaporated skim milk and extract. Add to dry ingredients. Mix lightly. Knead slightly on lightly floured board. Roll out to ½-inch thickness. Use 2½-inch biscuit cutter to cut out 8 biscuits. Place biscuits on baking sheet and bake for 10 minutes or until slightly brown on top. Meanwhile, in food processor or blender, process cottage cheese, 1½ teaspoons sugar and lemon juice. Fold in remaining ¼ cup raspberries. Split each warm biscuit in half. Place bottom halves in each of 8 individual serving dishes. Top with half the cottage cheese mixture and reserved sugared raspberries. Top with remaining biscuit halves, cottage cheese mixture and raspberries.

Nutrients per serving:			
Calories	166	Sodium	190 mg
Fat	2 g	Cholesterol	1 mg

Favorite recipe from **The Sugar Association**.

Harvest Bundt® Cake

Low Cholesterol

Makes 16 servings

2½ cups all-purpose flour
  1 tablespoon baking powder
  2 teaspoons ground cinnamon
1½ teaspoons baking soda
1½ cups boiling water
1½ cups NABISCO® 100% Bran™
  1 cup firmly packed light brown sugar
  1 cup seedless raisins
  ½ cup margarine, melted
  1 cup MOTT'S® Regular Apple Sauce
  2 eggs, slightly beaten

In medium bowl, mix flour, baking powder, cinnamon and baking soda; set aside. In large separate bowl, combine water, bran, brown sugar, raisins and margarine; let stand 5 minutes. Stir in apple sauce, eggs and flour mixture. Spoon into greased and floured 12-cup fluted tube pan. Bake at 350°F for 55 to 65 minutes or until toothpick inserted in center comes out clean. Cool in pan 10 minutes. Remove from pan; cool on wire rack.

Nutrients per serving:			
Calories	242	Sodium	272 mg
Fat	7 g	Cholesterol	27 mg

Chocolate Cake

Low Cholesterol

Makes 12 servings

  1 package DUNCAN HINES® Moist Deluxe Butter Recipe Fudge Cake Mix
  6 egg whites
  1 cup water
  ¼ cup PURITAN® Oil
    Confectioners sugar (optional)

1. Preheat oven to 375°F. Oil and flour 13×9×2-inch baking pan.

2. Combine cake mix, egg whites, water and oil in large bowl. Beat at low speed of electric mixer 4 minutes. Pour batter into pan. Bake at 375°F for 28 to 32 minutes or until wooden pick inserted in center comes out clean. Cool. Sprinkle with confectioners sugar, if desired.

Nutrients per serving:			
Calories	230	Sodium	265 mg
Fat	10 g	Cholesterol	0 mg

Mini Almond Cheesecakes

Mini Almond Cheesecakes

Under 200 Calories

Makes 12 servings

¾ cup ground almonds
1 tablespoon PARKAY® Margarine, melted
1 envelope unflavored gelatin
¼ cup cold water
1 (12 oz.) container PHILADELPHIA BRAND®
    LIGHT Pasteurized Process Cream Cheese
    Product
¾ cup skim milk
½ cup sugar or 12 packets sugar substitute
¼ teaspoon almond extract
3 cups peeled peach slices

• Stir together almonds and margarine in small bowl. Press mixture evenly onto bottoms of twelve paper-lined baking cups.

• Soften gelatin in water in small saucepan; stir over low heat until dissolved.

• Beat cream cheese product, milk, sugar and almond extract in large mixing bowl at medium speed with electric mixer until well blended. Stir in gelatin. Pour into baking cups; freeze until firm.

• Place peaches in food processor or blender container; process until smooth. Spoon peach purée onto individual plates.

• Remove cheesecakes from freezer 10 minutes before serving. Peel off paper. Invert cheesecakes onto plates. Garnish with additional peach slices, raspberries and fresh mint leaves, if desired.

Note: For a sweeter peach purée, add sugar to taste.

Nutrients per serving:			
Calories	175	Sodium	180 mg
Fat	10 g	Cholesterol	11 mg

Blueberry Angel Food Cake Roll

Blueberry Angel Food Cake Rolls

Makes 16 servings

1 package DUNCAN HINES® Angel Food
   Cake Mix
   Confectioners sugar
1 can (21 ounces) blueberry pie filling
¼ cup confectioners sugar

1. Preheat oven to 350°F. Line two 15½×10½×1-inch jelly-roll pans with aluminum foil.

2. Prepare cake following package directions. Divide batter into lined pans. Spread evenly. Cut through batter with knife or spatula to remove large air bubbles. Bake at 350°F for 15 minutes or until set. Invert cakes at once onto towels dusted with confectioners sugar. Remove foil carefully. Roll up each cake with towel jelly-roll fashion, starting at short end. Cool completely.

3. Unroll cakes. Spread about 1 cup blueberry pie filling to within 1 inch of edges on each cake. Reroll and place seam-side down on serving plate. Dust with ¼ cup confectioners sugar.

Nutrients per serving:			
Calories	143	Sodium	77 mg
Fat	0 g	Cholesterol	0 mg

Golden Apple Cupcakes

Makes 24 cupcakes

1 (18- to 20-ounce) package yellow cake mix
1 cup MOTT'S® Chunky Apple Sauce
⅓ cup vegetable oil
3 eggs
¼ cup firmly packed light brown sugar
¼ cup chopped walnuts
½ teaspoon ground cinnamon

In bowl, combine cake mix, apple sauce, oil and eggs; blend according to package directions. Spoon batter into 24 paper-lined muffin-pan cups. Mix brown sugar, walnuts and cinnamon; sprinkle over batter. Bake at 350°F for 20 to 25 minutes or until toothpick inserted in center comes out clean. Cool in pan 10 minutes. Remove from pan; cool on wire rack.

Nutrients per cupcake:			
Calories	157	Sodium	146 mg
Fat	6 g	Cholesterol	27 mg

Banana Upside-Down Cake

Makes 9 servings

3 tablespoons margarine
½ cup brown sugar, packed
4 firm, medium DOLE® Bananas, peeled,
   divided
1 egg
½ cup granulated sugar
3 tablespoons vegetable oil
2 tablespoons milk
1 teaspoon vanilla extract
½ teaspoon DOLE® Orange zest
1 cup all-purpose flour
1 teaspoon baking powder
½ teaspoon ground cinnamon
¼ teaspoon baking soda
⅛ teaspoon salt

• Melt margarine in 9-inch square cake pan 2 to 3 minutes as oven preheats to 350°F. Remove pan from oven; stir in brown sugar.

• Slice 3 of the bananas; arrange in single layer in brown sugar mixture. Cut remaining banana in chunks. Place banana chunks, egg, granulated sugar, oil, milk, vanilla and orange zest in food processor or blender. Process until smooth.

• Combine flour, baking powder, cinnamon, baking soda and salt in large bowl. Add banana mixture to dry mixture. Stir until blended. Pour batter over bananas in cake pan.

• Bake in 350°F oven 30 minutes or until cake tester inserted in center comes out clean. Cool in pan on wire rack 5 minutes. Invert onto serving plate. Serve warm or cool.

Nutrients per serving:			
Calories	271	Sodium	137 mg
Fat	9 g	Cholesterol	31 mg

Carrot Pudding Cake with Lemon Sauce

Heat oven to 325°F. Lightly spray 1½- or 2-qt. casserole with no-stick cooking spray or oil lightly. Combine ¼ cup margarine and brown sugar. Add apple juice concentrate and egg whites, mixing well. Add combined oat bran, flour, baking powder and cinnamon; mix well. Stir in carrots; pour into prepared dish. Bake 45 to 50 minutes or until edges are lightly browned and center is firm. Cool on wire rack about 1 hour.

Combine granulated sugar and cornstarch. Gradually add water, mixing until sugar dissolves. Cook over medium heat about 3 minutes, stirring constantly or until thickened and clear. Remove from heat; stir in remaining ingredients. Spoon 2 tablespoons lemon sauce over each serving.

Microwave Lemon Sauce Directions: In 4-cup microwavable measuring cup, combine granulated sugar and cornstarch. Gradually add water, mixing until sugar dissolves. Microwave at HIGH 2 to 3 minutes or until sauce is clear and thickened, stirring after every minute. Add remaining ingredients, mixing well. Cool slightly.

Nutrients per serving:

Calories	270	Sodium	200 mg
Fat	8 g	Cholesterol	0 mg

Carrot Pudding Cake with Lemon Sauce

Low Cholesterol

Makes 8 servings

¼ cup liquid vegetable oil margarine
⅓ cup firmly packed brown sugar
½ cup frozen apple juice concentrate, thawed
3 egg whites, slightly beaten
1 cup QUAKER® Oat Bran hot cereal, uncooked
½ cup all-purpose flour
2 teaspoons baking powder
1 teaspoon ground cinnamon
2 cups shredded carrots (about 4 or 5 medium)
½ cup granulated sugar
4 teaspoons cornstarch
1 cup hot water
1 tablespoon liquid vegetable oil margarine
1 tablespoon lemon juice
½ teaspoon grated lemon peel
1 drop yellow food coloring (optional)

Peachy Chocolate Cake

Under 200 Calories

Makes 12 servings

1½ cups all-purpose flour
1 cup sugar
¼ cup HERSHEY'S® Cocoa
1 teaspoon baking soda
½ teaspoon salt
1 cup water
¼ cup vegetable oil
1 tablespoon white vinegar
1 teaspoon vanilla extract
2 cups peeled, sliced fresh peaches, divided

Heat oven to 350°F. Grease and flour two 8-inch round baking pans. In large bowl, stir together flour, sugar, cocoa, baking soda and salt. Add water, oil, vinegar and vanilla. Beat with wire whisk or spoon just until batter is smooth and ingredients are well blended. Pour into prepared pans. Bake 20 to 25 minutes or until wooden pick inserted in center comes out clean. Cool 10 minutes; remove from pans to wire racks. Cool completely. Just before serving, place one cake layer on serving plate; arrange 1 cup of the peaches on layer. Top with second cake layer and remaining 1 cup peaches. Cut into slices; serve immediately.

Nutrients per serving:

Calories	181	Sodium	181 mg
Fat	5 g	Cholesterol	0 mg

Ginger Cake with Yogurt-Rum Sauce

Low Sodium

Makes 12 servings

Ginger Cake
- 2 cups all-purpose flour
- 2 teaspoons ground cinnamon
- 1¾ teaspoons ground ginger
- 1½ teaspoons ground nutmeg
- ¾ teaspoon baking powder
- ¾ teaspoon baking soda
- ½ teaspoon ground cloves
- ⅛ teaspoon salt
- ¾ cup molasses
- 2 large eggs
- 6 tablespoons light olive or vegetable oil
- ¼ cup granulated sugar
- ½ cup DANNON® Vanilla Lowfat Yogurt
- ½ cup boiling water

Yogurt-Rum Sauce
- ½ cup DANNON® Vanilla Lowfat Yogurt
- 4 teaspoons confectioners sugar
- ¾ teaspoon dark rum

To make cake, heat oven to 350°. Spray an 8-inch square baking pan with vegetable cooking spray. In large bowl, stir together flour, cinnamon, ginger, nutmeg, baking powder, baking soda, cloves and salt.

In medium bowl, combine molasses, eggs, oil and granulated sugar. Beat with wire whisk until well blended. Whisk in yogurt, then boiling water. Pour half the molasses mixture into dry ingredients and stir just until dry ingredients are moistened. Add the remaining molasses mixture; stir just until blended. (Batter will be slightly lumpy.) Pour batter into prepared pan.

Bake 45 to 55 minutes, until cake is springy to the touch and toothpick inserted in the center comes out clean. (Cake will form cracks on surface.) Cool on wire rack at least 30 minutes before serving. Flavor will improve on standing.

To make sauce, combine yogurt, confectioners sugar and rum in small bowl. Cut cake into 12 pieces; spoon sauce over each serving.

Nutrients per serving (includes 2 teaspoons sauce):			
Calories	275	Sodium	140 mg
Fat	8 g	Cholesterol	45 mg

Chocolate Angel Food Cake

Under 200 Calories

Makes 12 servings

One 14.5-oz to 16-oz. pkg. angel food cake mix, plus
    ingredients to prepare mix
½ cup NESTLÉ® Cocoa
    Confectioners' sugar, for garnish
    Strawberries, optional

Preheat oven according to cake mix directions. Combine cake mix (or cake flour) and cocoa. Prepare, bake and cool angel food cake according to cake mix directions. Sift confectioners' sugar over top of cake; serve with strawberries, if desired.

Nutrients per serving:			
Calories	157	Sodium	142 mg
Fat	1 g	Cholesterol	0 mg

Chocolate Angel Food Cake

Light 'n Luscious Cheesecake

Low Cholesterol

Makes 8 servings

1 tablespoon graham cracker crumbs
1 cup (8 ounces) lowfat cottage cheese
1 cup (8 ounces) plain lowfat yogurt
½ cup HELLMANN'S® or BEST FOODS®
    Light or Cholesterol Free Reduced Calorie
    Mayonnaise
⅓ cup sugar
2 teaspoons grated lemon peel
1 tablespoon lemon juice
1 teaspoon vanilla
2 egg whites
    Raspberry Sauce (recipe follows)
    Fresh raspberries for garnish (optional)

Grease 8-inch springform pan; dust with graham cracker crumbs. In blender or food processor container spoon cottage cheese. Process until smooth. Add yogurt, mayonnaise, sugar, lemon peel, lemon juice and vanilla; process until smooth. Add egg whites; process until well mixed. Pour into prepared pan. Bake in 325°F oven 30 minutes. Turn off oven. Leave cheesecake in oven with door ajar 30 minutes. Cool in pan on wire rack. Cover; chill several hours. Before serving, remove side of pan. Serve with Raspberry Sauce. If desired, garnish with fresh raspberries.

Raspberry Sauce: In blender or food processor, purée 1 package (10 ounces) frozen raspberries, thawed; strain. Stir in ⅓ cup Karo® Light or Dark Corn Syrup. *Makes about 2½ cups.*

Nutrients per serving:

Calories	209	Sodium	313 mg
Fat	5 g	Cholesterol	9 mg

Tropical Banana Cake

Low Cholesterol

Makes 16 servings

½ cup CRISCO® Shortening
1¾ cups sugar
2 eggs
1 egg white
½ cup skim milk
1½ teaspoons vanilla
1 cup mashed banana (about 2 medium)
1 can (8 ounces) crushed pineapple in
    unsweetened pineapple juice, undrained
3 cups all-purpose flour
1¼ teaspoons ground cinnamon
1 teaspoon baking soda
½ teaspoon salt
1 tablespoon finely chopped pecans

1. Heat oven to 350°F. Oil and flour 10-inch tube pan.

2. Combine Crisco and sugar in large bowl. Beat at medium speed of electric mixer until blended. Add eggs and egg white. Beat until light and fluffy. Add milk, vanilla, banana and pineapple with juice. Beat at low speed until mixed. (Batter will appear slightly curdled.)

3. Combine flour, cinnamon, baking soda and salt in separate bowl. Add to creamed mixture. Beat at low speed until mixed. Pour into pan. Sprinkle with nuts.

4. Bake at 350°F for 1 hour 10 minutes or until wooden pick inserted near center comes out clean. Cool in pan 25 minutes. Remove from pan. Cool completely on rack.

Nutrients per serving:

Calories	251	Sodium	134 mg
Fat	7 g	Cholesterol	27 mg

Orange Lover's Cake

Low Cholesterol

Makes 12 servings

1¼ cups granulated sugar
½ cup (1 stick) margarine
2 eggs
½ cup orange juice
½ cup water
2 teaspoons grated orange peel
1¾ cups all-purpose flour
1 cup QUAKER® Oats (Quick or Old Fashioned,
    uncooked)
2 teaspoons baking powder
½ teaspoon baking soda
½ teaspoon salt (optional)
½ cup powdered sugar
3 to 4 teaspoons orange juice
1 teaspoon grated orange peel

Heat oven to 350°F. Lightly spray 10-inch tube pan° with no-stick cooking spray or oil lightly. Beat granulated sugar, margarine and eggs until fluffy. Blend in ½ cup orange juice, water and 2 teaspoons orange peel; mix well. Add combined flour, oats, baking powder, baking soda and salt; mix well. Pour into prepared pan. Bake 45 to 50 minutes or until golden brown. Cool 10 minutes in pan; remove to wire rack. Cool completely. Combine remaining ingredients, mixing until smooth. Drizzle over completely cooled cake. Store loosely covered.

°Or use greased Bundt® pan. Decrease baking time by 5 minutes; increase cooling time to 30 minutes before removing from pan.

Nutrients per serving:

Calories	280	Sodium	300 mg
Fat	9 g	Cholesterol	45 mg

Light 'n Luscious Cheesecake

Lemony Light Vineyard "Cheesecakes"

Chocolate Raspberry Cheesecake

Makes 12 servings

  3 squares BAKER'S® Semi-Sweet Chocolate
  ¼ cup water
  1 (8 oz.) container PHILADELPHIA BRAND®
     Light Pasteurized Process Cream Cheese
     Product
  ½ cup light or low calorie raspberry fruit spread,
     divided
3¼ cups (8 ounces) COOL WHIP® LITE Whipped
     Topping, thawed, divided
  2 tablespoons water
36 fresh raspberries
  2 chocolate wafers, crushed

MICROWAVE° chocolate with ¼ cup water in large microwavable bowl at HIGH 1 to 1½ minutes until almost melted; stir until completely melted. (Mixture will be thick.)

BEAT chocolate, cream cheese product and ¼ cup of the fruit spread. Immediately stir in 2½ cups whipped topping until smooth. Spread in 8- or 9-inch pie plate or springform pan. Freeze 3 to 4 hours.

REMOVE from freezer; let stand 15 minutes. Briefly heat and stir remaining fruit spread and 2 tablespoons water until well blended. Remove from heat. Garnish each serving with fruit spread mixture, remaining whipped topping, raspberries and cookie crumbs. Store leftover cheesecake in freezer.

°*Range Top: Heat chocolate with water in saucepan over very low heat; stir constantly until just melted. Remove from heat; continue as above.*

Nutrients per serving:

Calories	139	Sodium	135 mg
Fat	8 g	Cholesterol	10 mg

Lemony Light Vineyard "Cheesecakes"

Makes 6 servings

  1 envelope unflavored gelatin
  ½ cup cold water
  1 package (8 ounces) light cream cheese,
     softened
  1 cup plain lowfat yogurt
  ⅓ cup sugar
  1 tablespoon grated lemon peel
  1 tablespoon lemon juice
  ¼ teaspoon vanilla
  4 ice cubes
1½ cups seedless, or halved seeded Chilean grapes

In small saucepan, sprinkle gelatin over cold water; let stand 1 minute to soften. Warm over low heat to dissolve. Combine in blender softened gelatin, cream cheese, yogurt, sugar, lemon peel, lemon juice and vanilla. Blend until smooth, scraping sides as needed. Add ice cubes; blend until smooth. Divide grapes between six (6-ounce) custard cups or individual dessert dishes. Pour cheese mixture over each, dividing equally. Chill until set. Garnish with additional grated lemon peel, if desired.

Nutrients per serving:

Calories	97	Sodium	141 mg
Fat	2 g	Cholesterol	6 mg

Favorite recipe from **Chilean Winter Fruit Association**.

Apple Chiffon Cake

Makes 12 servings

Cake

- ⅓ cup PURITAN® Oil
- ¾ cup sugar
- 2 eggs
- ¾ cup all-purpose flour
- ½ teaspoon baking powder
- ¼ teaspoon salt
- ¼ teaspoon baking soda
- ¼ teaspoon ground nutmeg
- ¼ teaspoon ground ginger
- 1 cup finely chopped peeled apples (2 small to medium)

Topping

- 2 tablespoons sugar
- 2 tablespoons finely chopped walnuts
- ½ teaspoon ground cinnamon

1. Heat oven to 350°F.

2. **For Cake**, combine Puritan® Oil and sugar in large bowl. Beat at medium speed of electric mixer until mixed. Add eggs; beat well.

3. Combine flour, baking powder, salt, baking soda, nutmeg and ginger in small bowl. Add to oil mixture. Beat just until blended. Stir in apples. Spread in ungreased 9-inch square pan.

4. **For Topping**, combine sugar, nuts and cinnamon in small bowl. Sprinkle over batter. Bake at 350°F for 25 to 30 minutes or until wooden pick inserted in center comes out clean. Cut into 3×2¼-inch rectangles. Serve warm or at room temperature.

Nutrients per serving:			
Calories	162	Sodium	86 mg
Fat	8 g	Cholesterol	36 mg

Tropical Fruit Delight

Makes 16 servings

Cake

- 1 package DUNCAN HINES® DeLights Lemon Cake Mix
- ½ cup CITRUS HILL® Orange Juice
- 2 eggs
- 1 tablespoon grated orange peel
  Confectioners sugar

Topping

- 1 can (11 ounces) mandarin orange segments
- 1 can (8 ounces) crushed pineapple with juice
- ¼ cup granulated sugar
- 1 tablespoon cornstarch
- 1 tablespoon butter or margarine (optional)
- 1 banana, sliced

1. Preheat oven to 350°F. Grease and flour 10-inch Bundt® pan.

2. **For Cake**, empty mix into large bowl. Add water to orange juice to equal 1⅓ cups. Add orange juice mixture, eggs and orange peel to mix. Prepare, bake and cool following package directions. Sift confectioners sugar over cooled cake.

3. **For Topping**, drain mandarin oranges, reserving juice. Drain pineapple, reserving juice. Combine juices in 1 cup measure. Add water or orange juice to fruit juices to equal 1 cup. Pour into small saucepan.

4. Combine granulated sugar and cornstarch. Stir into liquid. Cook on medium heat, stirring constantly, until thickened. Add butter, if desired. Stir until melted. Cool.

5. Stir oranges, pineapple and banana into cooled sauce. Cut cake into 16 servings. Spoon sauce over each serving. Sprinkle with coconut, if desired.

Nutrients per serving:			
Calories	209	Sodium	228 mg
Fat	5 g	Cholesterol	53 mg

Tropical Fruit Delight

Light Mocha Cake with Raspberry Sauce

Under 200 Calories

Makes about 24 servings

2 cups all-purpose flour
1¼ cups granulated sugar
½ cup NESTLÉ® Cocoa
2 teaspoons baking soda
1 teaspoon baking powder
½ teaspoon salt
1 cup buttermilk
1 cup hot coffee
⅔ cup vegetable oil
1 teaspoon vanilla extract
    Confectioners' sugar
    Raspberry Sauce (recipe follows)
    Low-calorie whipped topping, optional

Preheat oven to 350°F. Grease and flour 13×9-inch baking pan. In large mixer bowl, combine flour, granulated sugar, cocoa, baking soda, baking powder and salt. Gradually beat in buttermilk, coffee, oil and vanilla extract; continue beating until well blended. Pour into prepared pan.

Bake 35 to 40 minutes or until wooden toothpick inserted in center comes out clean. Cool completely. Sprinkle with confectioners' sugar. Cut into 2-inch squares. Top with Raspberry Sauce and whipped topping.

Raspberry Sauce: In blender or food processor, purée one 10-ounce pkg. frozen raspberries, thawed, until smooth. Press through fine sieve to remove seeds. In small saucepan, combine ½ cup water and 2 tablespoons cornstarch. Stir in purée. Bring to a boil over medium heat, stirring constantly. Boil 1 minute, stirring constantly. Cool completely.

Nutrients per serving:

Calories	156	Sodium	139 mg
Fat	6 g	Cholesterol	0 mg

Orange Poppy Seed Cake

Low Cholesterol

Makes 16 servings

1 (8 oz.) container PHILADELPHIA BRAND® LIGHT Pasteurized Process Cream Cheese Product
⅓ cup PARKAY® Margarine
1 cup sugar
3 eggs, separated
2 cups flour
1 teaspoon CALUMET® Baking Powder
1 teaspoon baking soda
1 cup BREAKSTONE'S® LIGHT CHOICE® Sour Half and Half
2 tablespoons poppy seeds
1 tablespoon grated orange peel
½ cup sugar or 12 packets sugar substitute
½ cup orange juice
3 tablespoons powdered sugar

• Preheat oven to 350°.

• Beat cream cheese product, margarine and 1 cup sugar in large mixing bowl at medium speed with electric mixer until well blended. Add egg yolks, one at a time, mixing well after each addition.

• Mix together flour, baking powder and baking soda; add to cream cheese mixture alternately with sour half and half. Stir in poppy seeds and orange peel.

• Beat egg whites in small mixing bowl at high speed with electric mixer until stiff peaks form; fold into cream cheese mixture. Pour into greased 10-inch fluted tube pan.

• Bake 50 minutes.

• Stir together ½ cup sugar and orange juice in saucepan over low heat until sugar dissolves. Prick hot cake several times with fork. Pour syrup over cake; cool 10 minutes. Invert onto serving plate. Cool completely. Sprinkle with powdered sugar. Garnish with quartered orange slices, if desired.

Nutrients per serving:

Calories	228	Sodium	157 mg
Fat	9 g	Cholesterol	48 mg

Orange Poppy Seed Cake

Creamy Citrus Cheesecake

Under 200 Calories

Makes 8 servings

¾ cup crushed graham crackers
2 tablespoons margarine, melted
3 eggs
½ cup sugar
1 teaspoon finely shredded orange peel
¼ cup orange juice
3 teaspoons vanilla, divided
2 (8-ounce) packages light cream cheese
1 cup DANNON® Plain, Lemon or Vanilla
    Lowfat Yogurt, divided
2 tablespoons powdered sugar

In bowl combine graham crackers and margarine. Press onto bottom of 7- or 8-inch springform pan. Bake at 325° for 6 minutes; let cool.

In a blender, combine eggs, sugar, orange peel, orange juice and 2 teaspoons of the vanilla. Cut cream cheese into chunks; add to mixture and blend until smooth. Stir in ½ cup of the yogurt. Pour into crust. Bake at 325° for 50 to 60 minutes or until nearly set.

Combine remaining ½ cup yogurt, the powdered sugar and remaining 1 teaspoon vanilla. Spread over hot cheesecake. Loosen sides of pan. Cool on wire rack. Chill before serving. Garnish with orange peel, if desired.

Nutrients per serving:

Calories	186	Sodium	286 mg
Fat	8 g	Cholesterol	88 mg

New England Streusel Cake

Low Cholesterol

Makes 16 servings

1½ cups NABISCO® 100% Bran™
1 cup MOTT'S® Regular Apple Sauce
1 cup milk
1 cup maple-flavored syrup
½ cup margarine, melted
2 eggs, slightly beaten
2½ cups all-purpose flour
1 tablespoon baking powder
1 teaspoon baking soda
1 teaspoon ground cinnamon
    Streusel Topping (recipe follows)

In large bowl, mix bran, apple sauce, milk, syrup, margarine and eggs; let stand 5 minutes. In separate bowl, blend flour, baking powder, baking soda and cinnamon; stir in bran mixture. Spread batter into greased 13×9×2-inch baking pan. Sprinkle with Streusel Topping. Bake at 350°F for 45 to 50 minutes or until toothpick inserted in center comes out clean. Cool completely in pan on wire rack.

Streusel Topping: In medium bowl, with electric mixer, beat ¼ cup margarine and ¼ cup sugar until creamy. Stir in 1 cup Nabisco® 100% Bran™, ¼ cup all-purpose flour and ½ teaspoon ground cinnamon.

Nutrients per serving:

Calories	279	Sodium	308 mg
Fat	10 g	Cholesterol	29 mg

Creamy Citrus Cheesecake

Golden Carrot Cake

Low Cholesterol

Makes 12 servings

Cake

- 1 cup all-purpose flour
- ½ teaspoon salt
- ½ teaspoon baking soda
- ½ teaspoon baking powder
- 1 teaspoon cinnamon
- ¼ teaspoon nutmeg
- 1 can (8 ounces) crushed pineapple, undrained
- 2 eggs
- 1 cup firmly packed brown sugar
- ⅓ cup vegetable oil
- 1½ cups shredded raw carrots
- ½ cup chopped walnuts (optional)
- 2 cups KELLOGG'S® RAISIN BRAN cereal

Frosting

- 2 tablespoons reserved pineapple juice
- 1 cup confectioners sugar

1. **To make Cake,** stir together flour, salt, baking soda, baking powder and spices; set aside.

2. Drain pineapple, reserving 2 tablespoons pineapple juice for frosting.

3. In large mixing bowl, beat together eggs, brown sugar and oil. Stir in carrots, pineapple, walnuts and Kellogg's® Raisin Bran cereal. Add dry ingredients, mixing until well combined. Pour into greased 9-inch square baking pan.

4. Bake in 350°F oven about 40 minutes or until wooden pick inserted near center comes out clean.

5. **To make Frosting,** combine reserved pineapple juice and confectioners sugar until smooth. Spread evenly over hot cake. Cool completely and store in refrigerator.

Nutrients per serving:			
Calories	280	Sodium	220 mg
Fat	10 g	Cholesterol	46 mg

Chocolate Orange Delight

Chocolate Orange Delight

Under 200 Calories

Makes 16 servings

Cake

- 1 package DUNCAN HINES® DeLights Devil's Food Cake Mix
- 1 tablespoon grated orange peel

Topping

- 1 container (8 ounces) frozen whipped topping, thawed
- 2 tablespoons CITRUS HILL® Frozen Orange Juice Concentrate, thawed
- Orange slices, for garnish

1. Preheat oven to 350°F. Grease and flour 13×9×2-inch pan.

2. **For Cake,** add orange peel to mix. Prepare, bake and cool following package directions.

3. **For Topping,** combine whipped topping and orange juice concentrate in medium bowl. Stir until blended. Spoon dollop of topping on each cake serving. Garnish with orange slices. Refrigerate leftover topping.

Tip: To make orange juice from remaining concentrate, measure remaining concentrate; add 3 times the amount of water to concentrate.

Nutrients per serving:			
Calories	193	Sodium	271 mg
Fat	7 g	Cholesterol	52 mg

Deep-Dish Peach Pie

Pleasing

PIES

Deep-Dish Peach Pie

Low Cholesterol

Makes 8 servings

> Pastry for 1-crust pie
> 1 cup sugar
> 2 tablespoons cornstarch
> 3 pounds peaches, seeded, pared and sliced
>   (about 6 cups)
> 2 tablespoons REALEMON® Lemon Juice from
>   Concentrate
> 1 tablespoon margarine, melted
> ¼ teaspoon almond extract
> 2 tablespoons sliced almonds

Preheat oven to 375°. Remove and reserve *1 tablespoon* sugar. In small bowl, combine remaining sugar and cornstarch. In large bowl, toss peaches with ReaLemon® brand; add sugar mixture, margarine and extract. Turn into 8-inch square baking dish. Roll pastry to 9-inch square; cut slits near center. Place pastry over filling; turn under edges, seal and flute. Sprinkle with reserved *1 tablespoon* sugar and almonds. Bake 45 to 50 minutes or until golden brown.

Nutrients per serving:

Calories	292	Sodium	163 mg
Fat	10 g	Cholesterol	0 mg

Fruit Lover's Tart

Low Cholesterol

Makes 8 servings

> 1¼ cups QUAKER® Oats (Quick or Old Fashioned,
>   uncooked)
> ⅓ cup firmly packed brown sugar
> ¼ cup all-purpose flour
> 2 tablespoons margarine, melted
> 2 egg whites
> 1 cup (8 ounces) part-skim ricotta cheese
> ¼ cup (2 ounces) light cream cheese, softened
> 2 tablespoons powdered sugar
> ½ teaspoon grated lemon peel
> 4½ cups any combination sliced fresh or frozen
>   fruit, thawed, well drained

Heat oven to 350°F. Lightly spray 9-inch pie plate with no-stick cooking spray or oil lightly. Combine oats, brown sugar, flour, margarine and egg whites, mixing until moistened. Press mixture onto bottom of prepared plate. Bake 15 to 18 minutes or until light golden brown. Remove to wire rack; cool completely. Combine cheeses, powdered sugar and lemon peel. Spread onto oat base; top with fruit. Chill 2 hours.

Microwave Directions: Combine oats, brown sugar, flour, margarine and egg whites, mixing until moistened. Press mixture onto bottom of 9-inch microwave-safe pie plate. Microwave on HIGH 2 minutes 30 seconds to 3 minutes or until top springs back when lightly touched. Cool completely. Proceed as above.

Nutrients per serving:

Calories	240	Sodium	110 mg
Fat	8 g	Cholesterol	15 mg

Cranberry Apple Pie with Soft Gingersnap Crust

Under 200 Calories

Makes 8 servings

20 gingersnap cookies
1½ tablespoons margarine
2 McIntosh apples, pared and cored
1 cup fresh cranberries
5 tablespoons dark brown sugar
¼ teaspoon vanilla extract
¼ teaspoon ground cinnamon
1 teaspoon granulated sugar

Preheat oven to 375°F. Place gingersnaps and margarine in food processor; process until finely ground. Press gingersnap mixture into 8-inch pie plate. Bake 5 to 8 minutes; remove and cool crust. Chop apples in food processor. Add cranberries, brown sugar, vanilla and cinnamon; pulse just until mixed. Spoon apple-cranberry filling into another 8-inch pie plate or casserole dish. Sprinkle with granulated sugar. Bake 35 minutes or until tender. Spoon filling into gingersnap crust and serve immediately.

Nutrients per serving:

Calories	124	Sodium	90 mg
Fat	3 g	Cholesterol	0 mg

Favorite recipe from **The Sugar Association**.

Luscious Pumpkin Pie

Makes 8 servings

1 teaspoon water
1 egg white
1 (6-ounce) KEEBLER® Ready-Crust® Pie
   Crust, Graham or Butter
2 eggs
1½ cups pumpkin pie filling
8 ounces DANNON® Plain Lowfat Yogurt
1 cup evaporated milk
¾ cup sugar
1 teaspoon vanilla extract
1 teaspoon ground cinnamon
¼ teaspoon ground cloves
¼ teaspoon ground ginger
¼ teaspoon ground nutmeg

Beat together water and egg white. Brush onto Keebler® Ready-Crust®. Place on cookie sheet and bake 3 minutes in 375° oven. Crust should be lightly golden. Cool thoroughly.

In a large bowl, slightly beat 2 eggs. Add pumpkin pie filling, yogurt, evaporated milk, sugar, vanilla, cinnamon, cloves, ginger and nutmeg. Stir until thoroughly mixed.

Pour into pie crust. Place on cookie sheet and bake 60 minutes in 375° oven or until set. Cool completely. Serve with whipped cream if desired.

Nutrients per serving:

Calories	289	Sodium	327 mg
Fat	10 g	Cholesterol	64 mg

Cherry Yogurt Sesame Pie

Low Cholesterol

Makes 8 servings

Crust
   1 cup all-purpose flour
   2 tablespoons wheat germ
   2 tablespoons sesame seeds
   1 tablespoon sugar
   ⅓ cup butter or margarine
   4 tablespoons cold water

Filling
   1 envelope unflavored gelatin
   ¼ cup cold water
   1 carton (8 ounces) nonfat plain or lowfat vanilla
      yogurt
   1 can (21 ounces) cherry pie filling and topping

For Crust, place flour, wheat germ, sesame seeds and sugar in large mixing bowl. Cut in butter until mixture is size of small peas. Add 4 tablespoons water and mix with fork until dough just holds together. Form into a ball; flatten and roll out on floured surface to fit 9-inch pie pan. Fit dough into pan, flute edges and prick crust several times with fork. Bake at 450°F for 10 to 15 minutes or until golden brown. Cool completely.

For Filling, in large microwave-safe bowl, sprinkle gelatin over ¼ cup water; let stand 1 minute to soften. Microwave on full power (high) 10 seconds; stir until gelatin is dissolved. Whisk in yogurt, then gently fold in cherry pie filling. Spoon into cooled baked crust. Chill until firm, about 2 hours.

Nutrients per serving:

Calories	245	Sodium	104 mg
Fat	9 g	Cholesterol	22 mg

Favorite recipe from **New York Cherry Growers Association**.

Margarita Pie

Margarita Pie

Low Cholesterol

Makes 10 servings

1 envelope KNOX® Unflavored Gelatine
¼ cup cold skim milk
½ cup skim milk, heated to boiling
1 carton (8 ounces) cholesterol-free egg substitute
⅔ cup sugar
⅓ cup lime juice
2 to 3 tablespoons tequila
1 teaspoon grated lime peel
1 to 2 drops green food coloring (optional)
1 cup lite frozen whipped topping, thawed
1 9-inch baked pastry shell

In blender, sprinkle unflavored gelatine over cold milk; let stand 2 minutes. Add hot milk and process at low speed until gelatine is completely dissolved, about 2 minutes. Add egg substitute, sugar, lime juice, tequila, lime peel and food coloring. Process at high speed until thoroughly blended, about 1 minute. Pour into large bowl and chill, stirring occasionally with wire whisk, until mixture mounds slightly when dropped from spoon, about 1 hour. Fold in whipped topping. Pour into pastry shell; chill until firm, about 4 hours. Garnish, if desired, with additional whipped topping and lime slices.

Nutrients per serving:			
Calories	225	Sodium	177 mg
Fat	10 g	Cholesterol	1 mg

Mocha Dream Pie

Makes 10 servings

8 phyllo strudel sheets (12×17 inches each)
1 envelope KNOX® Unflavored Gelatine
½ cup cold skim milk
½ cup skim milk, heated to boiling
2 tablespoons unsweetened cocoa powder
2 teaspoons instant coffee
1 container (15 ounces) part-skim ricotta cheese
½ cup sugar
1 teaspoon vanilla extract
½ teaspoon ground cinnamon
¼ teaspoon salt

Preheat oven to 350°. Spray 9-inch pie plate with non-stick cooking spray; place on baking sheet. Place 4 phyllo strudel sheets across pie plate, extending sheets over sides; press gently into plate. Place remaining 4 sheets in opposite direction across pie plate, extending sheets over sides, to form cross; press gently into pie plate. With scissors, cut edge 1 inch beyond rim of plate; pierce crust with fork. Squeeze phyllo strudel trimmings into small bundles; place on baking sheet. Spray crust and bundles with cooking spray. Bake 15 minutes or until golden brown; cool on wire rack.

In blender, sprinkle unflavored gelatine over cold milk; let stand 2 minutes. Add hot milk, cocoa and instant coffee and process at low speed until completely dissolved, about 2 minutes. Add remaining ingredients and process at high speed until thoroughly blended, scraping sides once, about 2 minutes. Pour into prepared crust; chill until firm, at least 2 hours. Garnish with phyllo bundles.

Nutrients per serving:			
Calories	164	Sodium	188 mg
Fat	4 g	Cholesterol	14 mg

Picnic Fruit Tart

Makes 12 to 14 servings

¾ cup flour
¼ cup oat bran
2 tablespoons sugar
¼ cup PARKAY® Margarine
2 to 3 tablespoons cold water
1 envelope unflavored gelatin
½ cup cold water
1 (8 oz.) container PHILADELPHIA BRAND® LIGHT Pasteurized Process Cream Cheese Product
¼ cup sugar or 6 packets sugar substitute
1 teaspoon grated lemon peel
¼ cup skim milk
⅔ cup KRAFT® Apricot Preserves
¾ cup grape halves
¾ cup plum slices

• Preheat oven to 375°.

• Mix together flour, oat bran and 2 tablespoons sugar in medium bowl; cut in margarine until mixture resembles coarse crumbs. Sprinkle with 2 to 3 tablespoons water, mixing lightly with fork until just moistened. Roll into ball. Cover; chill.

• Roll out dough to 11-inch circle on lightly floured surface. Place in 9-inch tart pan with removable bottom. Trim edges; prick bottom with fork. Bake 16 to 18 minutes or until golden brown; cool.

• Soften gelatin in ½ cup cold water in small saucepan; stir over low heat until dissolved. Cool.

• Beat cream cheese product, ¼ cup sugar and lemon peel in large mixing bowl at medium speed with electric mixer until well blended. Gradually add gelatin and milk, mixing until well blended. Pour into crust. Chill until firm.

• Heat preserves in small saucepan over low heat until thinned. Spread evenly over tart. Arrange fruit over preserves. Carefully remove rim of pan.

Variation: To make individual tarts, prepare dough as directed. Divide dough into 14 equal portions; roll each into ball. Cover; chill. Roll each ball on lightly floured surface into 5-inch circle. Place in 3-inch tart pans; prick bottoms with fork. Bake 12 to 15 minutes or until lightly browned; cool. Continue as directed.

Nutrients per serving:			
Calories	150	Sodium	130 mg
Fat	6 g	Cholesterol	10 mg

Picnic Fruit Tart

Easy Pineapple Pie

Fresh Fruit Tart

Low Cholesterol

Makes 8 servings

3 cups cooked rice
¼ cup sugar
1 egg, beaten
  Vegetable cooking spray
1 package (8 ounces) light cream cheese, softened
¼ cup plain nonfat yogurt
¼ cup confectioner's sugar
1 teaspoon vanilla extract
⅓ cup low-sugar apricot or peach spread
1 tablespoon water
2 to 3 cups fresh fruit (sliced strawberries, raspberries, blueberries, sliced kiwifruit, grape halves)

Combine rice, sugar, and egg in medium bowl. Press into 12-inch pizza pan or 10-inch pie pan coated with cooking spray. Bake at 350°F. for 10 minutes. Cool.

Beat cream cheese and yogurt in medium bowl until light and fluffy. Add confectioner's sugar and vanilla; beat until well blended. Spread over crust.

Heat apricot spread and water in small saucepan over low heat. Strain; cool. Brush half of glaze over filling. Arrange fruit attractively over crust, starting at outer edge. Brush remaining glaze evenly over fruit. Cover and chill 1 to 2 hours before serving.

Nutrients per serving:

Calories	257	Sodium	432 mg
Fat	8 g	Cholesterol	48 mg

Favorite recipe from **USA Rice Council.**

Easy Pineapple Pie

Low Cholesterol

Makes 6 to 8 servings

1 can (20 ounces) DOLE® Crushed Pineapple in Syrup°
1 package (3.5 ounces) instant lemon pudding and pie filling mix
1 cup milk
1 carton (4 ounces) frozen whipped topping, thawed
2 tablespoons DOLE® Lemon juice
1 teaspoon DOLE® Lemon zest
1 (8- or 9-inch) graham cracker pie crust

- Drain pineapple well. Combine pudding mix and milk in medium bowl. Beat 2 to 3 minutes until very thick.

- Fold in whipped topping, pineapple, lemon juice and lemon zest. Pour into crust. Cover and refrigerate 4 hours or overnight. Garnish as desired.

°*Use pineapple packed in juice, if desired.*

Nutrients per serving:

Calories	266	Sodium	321 mg
Fat	10 g	Cholesterol	2 mg

Iced Coffee and Chocolate Pie

Low Cholesterol

Makes 8 servings

¼ cup cold skim milk
2 envelopes unflavored gelatin
1 cup skim milk, heated to boiling
2 cups vanilla ice milk
⅓ cup sugar
2 tablespoons instant coffee granules
1 teaspoon vanilla extract
1 (6-ounce) KEEBLER® Ready-Crust® Chocolate Flavored Pie Crust
  Reduced calorie whipped topping, optional
  Chocolate curls, optional

In blender container, add ¼ cup cold milk. Sprinkle gelatin over milk and mix on LOW. Let stand 3 to 4 minutes to soften. Add hot milk; cover and mix on LOW until gelatin dissolves, about 2 minutes. Add ice milk, sugar, coffee granules and vanilla. Cover and mix until smooth. Pour into crust. Chill at least 2 hours. Garnish with whipped topping and chocolate curls, if desired.

Nutrients per serving:

Calories	220	Sodium	210 mg
Fat	6 g	Cholesterol	6 mg

Frozen Yogurt Pie

Makes 8 servings

1¾ cups NABISCO® 100% Bran™, finely rolled
¼ cup firmly packed brown sugar
⅓ cup margarine, melted
1½ pints vanilla frozen lowfat yogurt, softened
1½ cups MOTT'S® Chunky Apple Sauce
½ teaspoon ground cinnamon
    Fresh fruit and mint sprigs for garnish, optional

In small bowl, combine bran, brown sugar and margarine. Press mixture on bottom and side of 9-inch pie plate. Bake at 375°F for 8 minutes; cool completely. In large bowl, blend frozen yogurt, apple sauce and cinnamon. Spread in cooled crust. Freeze 4 hours or until firm. Garnish with fruit and mint if desired.

Nutrients per serving:

Calories	249	Sodium	232 mg
Fat	9 g	Cholesterol	4 mg

Cranberry-Apple Tart

Makes 9 servings

Crust
  3 cups RALSTON® Brand Fruit & Nut Muesli with
      Cranberries, crushed to 2 cups
¼ cup (½ stick) margarine or butter, melted
¼ cup packed brown sugar

Filling
  2 cups cranberries, fresh or frozen
½ cup granulated sugar
½ cup water
  1 tablespoon lemon juice
  1 can (20 ounces) apple pie filling
    Shredded cheese and mint leaves, optional

To prepare Crust: Preheat oven to 350°. In medium bowl combine cereal, margarine and brown sugar. Press cereal mixture firmly into 9-inch fluted tart pan or 9-inch pie plate. Bake 7 to 8 minutes or until lightly browned. Cool completely.

To prepare Filling: In medium saucepan over medium heat combine cranberries, granulated sugar, water and lemon juice. Cook, stirring frequently, until mixture comes to a boil; reduce heat and simmer 15 to 18 minutes, stirring frequently. Remove from heat and cool completely. Pour apple pie filling into cooled crust; top with cooled cranberry mixture. Garnish with cheese and mint if desired.

Nutrients per serving:

Calories	288	Sodium	185 mg
Fat	7 g	Cholesterol	0 mg

Pumpkin Cheesecake Pie

Makes 10 servings

  1 cup gingersnap cookie crumbs
  1 tablespoon brown sugar
  3 tablespoons margarine, melted
  1 envelope KNOX® Unflavored Gelatine
¼ cup cold skim milk
½ cup skim milk, heated to boiling
  1 can (16 ounces) pumpkin (about 2 cups)
  1 package (8 ounces) lite cream cheese, softened
¾ cup packed brown sugar
  1 teaspoon vanilla extract
  1 teaspoon ground cinnamon
½ teaspoon salt
⅛ teaspoon ground cloves
  1 cup lite frozen whipped topping, thawed

In 9-inch pie plate, combine gingersnap crumbs and 1 tablespoon brown sugar. Drizzle with melted margarine. Pat crumbs into bottom and up side of pie plate to make crust; set aside. In blender, sprinkle unflavored gelatine over cold milk; let stand 2 minutes. Add hot milk and process at low speed until gelatine is completely dissolved, about 2 minutes. Add pumpkin, cream cheese, ¾ cup brown sugar, vanilla, cinnamon, salt and cloves. Process at high speed until thoroughly blended, scraping sides frequently, about 5 minutes. Pour into prepared crust. Chill until firm, about 3 hours. Top with whipped topping.

Nutrients per serving:

Calories	218	Sodium	267 mg
Fat	9 g	Cholesterol	4 mg

Pumpkin Cheesecake Pie

Light Custard Cheese Pie

Makes 6 servings

1 (9-inch) graham cracker crumb crust
1 (16-ounce) container BORDEN® Lite-line® or VIVA® Cottage Cheese
1 tablespoon REALEMON® Lemon Juice from Concentrate
3 eggs
⅓ cup sugar
⅓ cup BORDEN® Lite-line® or VIVA® Protein Fortified Skim Milk
1 teaspoon vanilla extract
1 cup assorted cut-up fresh fruit

Preheat oven to 350°F. In blender container, combine cottage cheese and ReaLemon® brand; blend until smooth. In large mixer bowl, beat eggs and sugar; add cheese mixture, milk and vanilla. Beat until smooth. Pour into crust. Bake 45 minutes or until set. Cool. Chill. Top with fresh fruit and serve. Refrigerate leftovers.

Nutrients per serving:			
Calories	288	Sodium	452 mg
Fat	10 g	Cholesterol	113 mg

Light Lemon Meringue Pie

Low Cholesterol

Makes 8 servings

Crust
1¼ cups all-purpose flour
½ teaspoon salt (optional)
⅓ cup CRISCO® Shortening
¼ cup CITRUS HILL® Orange Juice

Filling
1 cup sugar
⅓ cup cornstarch
⅛ teaspoon salt (optional)
1½ cups cold water
1 egg yolk, lightly beaten
1 teaspoon grated fresh lemon peel
⅓ cup fresh lemon juice

Meringue
3 egg whites
⅛ teaspoon salt (optional)
¼ cup sugar
½ teaspoon vanilla

1. Heat oven to 425°F.

2. **For Crust,** combine flour and salt (if used) in bowl. Cut in Crisco using pastry blender or 2 knives until all flour is blended in to form pea-sized chunks. Sprinkle orange juice over flour mixture 1 tablespoon at a time. Toss lightly with fork until dough forms. (Dough may seem slightly dry and crumbly.) Press into ball.

3. Press dough ball to form 5- to 6-inch "pancake." Roll between sheets of waxed paper until 1 inch larger than upside-down 9-inch pie plate. Peel off top sheet. Flip into pie plate. Remove other sheet. Fold dough edge under and flute. Prick bottom and sides with fork (50 times) to prevent shrinkage. Bake at 425°F for 10 to 15 minutes or until lightly browned.

4. **For Filling,** combine sugar, cornstarch and salt (if used) in heavy saucepan. Stir in water gradually, blending until smooth. Cook on medium-high heat, stirring constantly, until filling comes to a boil. Cook on medium heat, stirring constantly, 5 minutes. Remove from heat.

5. Stir small amount of hot mixture into egg yolk. Return mixture to saucepan. Cook, stirring, 1 minute. Remove from heat. Stir in lemon peel and juice. *Reduce oven temperature to 350°F.*

6. **For Meringue,** beat egg whites and salt (if used) until frothy. Add sugar gradually, beating well after each addition. Continue beating until stiff but not dry. Fold in vanilla.

7. **Spoon filling into baked pie crust. Spread meringue over filling, sealing meringue to edge of pie crust. Bake at 350°F for 15 minutes or until golden brown. Cool completely on wire rack. Cut with sharp knife dipped in hot water.

Nutrients per serving (with optional salt):			
Calories	289	Sodium	224 mg
Fat	9 g	Cholesterol	27 mg

Nutrients per serving (without optional salt):			
Calories	289	Sodium	24 mg
Fat	9 g	Cholesterol	27 mg

Pear Bistro Tart

Pear Bistro Tart

Low Sodium

Makes 10 servings

- ½ cup sugar
- ¼ cup cornstarch
- 2 eggs, slightly beaten
- 2 cups low-fat milk
- 1 teaspoon lemon zest
- ¼ teaspoon orange extract
  Baked 9-inch tart shell
- 2 fresh California Bartlett pears, pared, sliced
- ¼ cup apricot preserves, heated

Mix sugar and cornstarch in medium bowl; whisk in eggs. Scald milk; slowly whisk hot milk into egg mixture. Return to heat. Stir while cooking until thickened. Stir in lemon zest and orange extract; cool. Pour into baked tart shell. Arrange sliced pears on top; brush with hot apricot preserves.

Nutrients per serving:

Calories	214	Sodium	184 mg
Fat	8 g	Cholesterol	57 mg

Favorite recipe from **California Tree Fruit Agreement**.

Lite 'n Easy Crustless Pumpkin Pie

Under 100 Calories

Makes 10 servings

- 2 envelopes unflavored gelatin
- 2 tablespoons cold water
- 2¼ cups *undiluted* CARNATION® Lowfat Evaporated Milk, divided
- 1¾ cups (16-ounce can) LIBBY'S® Solid Pack Pumpkin
- 6 tablespoons packed dark brown sugar or low calorie sweetener equivalent
- 1 teaspoon pumpkin pie spice
- 1 teaspoon vanilla extract

In medium bowl, sprinkle gelatin over cold water to soften; set aside. In small saucepan, heat *1 cup* of the evaporated milk to just boiling. Slowly stir hot milk into gelatin; stir until gelatin is dissolved. Mix in *remaining* evaporated milk, the pumpkin, brown sugar, pumpkin pie spice, and vanilla; set aside. Spray 10-inch glass pie plate with non-stick vegetable coating. Pour mixture into pie plate; chill until firm.

Nutrients per serving:

Calories	97	Sodium	70 mg
Fat	2 g	Cholesterol	4 mg

Cocoa Brownies and Chocolate Chip Cookies

Cookie

MAGIC

Cocoa Brownies

Under 200 Calories

Makes 18 brownies

  4 egg whites
  ½ cup PURITAN® Oil
  1 teaspoon vanilla extract
1⅓ cups sugar
  ½ cup unsweetened cocoa
1¼ cups all-purpose flour
  ¼ teaspoon salt

1. Preheat oven to 350°F. Oil bottom of 9-inch square pan. Set aside.

2. Place egg whites in large bowl. Beat with spoon until slightly frothy. Add Puritan® Oil and vanilla. Mix thoroughly. Stir in sugar and cocoa. Mix well. Stir in flour and salt until blended. Pour into pan.

3. Bake at 350°F for 26 to 28 minutes or until brownies start to pull away from side of pan. *Do not overbake.* Cool completely. Cut into bars. Sprinkle with confectioners sugar, if desired.

Nutrients per brownie:			
Calories	150	Sodium	43 mg
Fat	7 g	Cholesterol	0 mg

Chocolate Chip Cookies

Under 100 Calories

Makes 3 dozen cookies

2 cups all-purpose flour
1 teaspoon baking soda
½ teaspoon salt
1 egg
3 tablespoons water
1 teaspoon vanilla extract
1 cup firmly packed brown sugar
¼ cup PURITAN® Oil
½ cup semi-sweet chocolate chips

1. Heat oven to 375°F. Oil baking sheets well. Combine flour, baking soda and salt. Set aside. Combine egg, water and vanilla. Set aside.

2. Blend brown sugar and Puritan® Oil in large bowl at low speed of electric mixer. Add egg mixture. Beat until smooth. Add flour mixture in three parts at lowest speed. Scrape bowl well after each addition. Stir in chocolate chips.

3. Drop dough by rounded teaspoonfuls onto baking sheets. Bake at 375°F for 7 to 8 minutes or until lightly browned. Cool on baking sheets 1 minute. Remove to cooling racks.

Nutrients per cookie:			
Calories	74	Sodium	57 mg
Fat	3 g	Cholesterol	6 mg

Spectacular Cannolis

Under 200 Calories

Makes 40 cookies

1 (8 oz.) container PHILADELPHIA BRAND® Soft Cream Cheese with Strawberries
2 tablespoons milk
2 (5½ oz.) boxes pirouette cookies
¾ cup BAKER'S® Real Semi-Sweet Chocolate Chips

- Blend cream cheese and milk in small bowl until smooth.

- Spoon cream cheese mixture into pastry bag; pipe into cookies. Chill 10 minutes.

- Melt chocolate chips in small saucepan over low heat, stirring constantly until smooth. Drizzle cookies with chocolate. Chill.

Nutrients per serving (2 cookies):			
Calories	180	Sodium	40 mg
Fat	4 g	Cholesterol	5 mg

Lemon Cookies

Lemon Cookies

Under 100 Calories

Makes 4 dozen cookies

⅔ cup MIRACLE WHIP® Salad Dressing
1 two-layer yellow cake mix
2 eggs
2 teaspoons grated lemon peel
⅔ cup ready-to-spread vanilla frosting
4 teaspoons lemon juice

• Preheat oven to 375°.

• Blend salad dressing, cake mix and eggs at low speed with electric mixer until moistened. Add lemon peel. Beat on medium speed 2 minutes. (Dough will be stiff.)

• Drop rounded teaspoonfuls of dough, 2 inches apart, onto greased cookie sheets.

• Bake 9 to 11 minutes or until lightly browned. (Cookies will still appear soft.) Cool 1 minute; remove from cookie sheets. Cool completely.

• Stir together frosting and juice until well blended. Spread on cookies.

Nutrients per cookie:

Calories	80	Sodium	100 mg
Fat	4 g	Cholesterol	10 mg

Double Delight Cookies

Under 100 Calories

Makes 3 dozen cookies

1 package DUNCAN HINES® DeLights Fudge Marble Cake Mix
2 eggs
¼ cup PURITAN® Oil

1. Preheat oven to 375°F. Grease baking sheets.

2. Combine cake mix, eggs and oil in large bowl. Stir until thoroughly blended. Divide dough in half. Blend cocoa packet from Mix into half of dough. Shape into balls using 1 measuring teaspoon.

3. For each cookie, place 2 chocolate and 2 yellow balls together with sides touching. Arrange 2 inches apart on baking sheets. Flatten slightly with bottom of glass. Bake at 375°F for 8 to 9 minutes or until set. Cool 1 minute on baking sheet. Remove to cooling rack to cool completely.

Nutrients per cookie:

Calories	78	Sodium	87 mg
Fat	3 g	Cholesterol	24 mg

Jelly-Filled Dainties

Under 100 Calories

Makes 4 dozen cookies

2 cups all-purpose flour
½ teaspoon salt
2¼ cups KELLOGG'S® CORN FLAKES cereal
1 cup margarine, softened
½ cup firmly packed brown sugar
1 egg
½ teaspoon vanilla extract
1 cup currant, raspberry or strawberry jelly

1. Stir together flour and salt; set aside. Crush Kellogg's® Corn Flakes cereal into fine crumbs, about ½ cup; set aside.

2. In large bowl, blend margarine and sugar. Add egg and vanilla; beat well. Stir in flour mixture.

3. Shape dough into 1-inch balls. Roll in cereal. Place about 2 inches apart on ungreased baking sheets. Make an indentation in each cookie using handle of wooden spoon.

4. Bake at 300°F for 8 to 10 minutes. Remove from oven; press down indentation in each cookie. Return to oven and bake about 10 minutes longer or until lightly browned. Cool on baking sheets 1 minute. Cool completely on wire racks. When cool, fill centers with about 1 teaspoon jelly.

Nutrients per cookie:

Calories	84	Sodium	82 mg
Fat	4 g	Cholesterol	4 mg

Almond Macaroons

Makes 3 dozen cookies

4 egg whites
⅔ cup sugar
One 12-oz. pkg. (2 cups) NESTLÉ® TOLL
   HOUSE® Semi-Sweet Chocolate Mini
   Morsels
1½ cups ground blanched almonds
½ teaspoon almond extract

Preheat oven to 350°F. Grease cookie sheets. In large mixer bowl, beat egg whites until foamy. Gradually add sugar, beating until stiff peaks form. Fold in mini morsels, almonds and almond extract. Drop by heaping measuring teaspoonfuls onto prepared cookie sheets.

Bake 20 minutes or until lightly browned and set. Let stand on cookie sheets 2 minutes. Remove from cookie sheets; cool.

Nutrients per cookie:

Calories	97	Sodium	7 mg
Fat	6 g	Cholesterol	0 mg

Apricot Nut Supreme Brownies

Makes 18 brownies

4 ounces white chocolate or white baking bars
⅓ cup butter or margarine
½ cup sugar
2 eggs
¼ teaspoon almond extract
¾ cup all-purpose flour
½ teaspoon baking powder
¼ teaspoon salt
1 cup Dried California Apricots, quartered and
   divided
½ cup slivered almonds, divided

Preheat oven to 350°F. In small saucepan, melt white chocolate and butter over low heat. Stir constantly until melted; remove from heat. Add sugar, eggs and extract; stir to blend. In separate bowl, combine flour, baking powder and salt. Stir into white chocolate mixture; add ½ cup of the apricots and ¼ cup of the almonds. Pour batter into greased 10½×7×1½-inch pan. Sprinkle top with remaining ½ cup apricots and ¼ cup almonds. Bake 25 minutes or until golden and brownies begin to pull away from edge of pan. Cool completely; cut into bars.

Nutrients per brownie:

Calories	120	Sodium	90 mg
Fat	6 g	Cholesterol	24 mg

Favorite recipe from **California Apricot Advisory Board.**

Tropical Bar Cookies

Makes 16 bars

½ cup DOLE® Sliced Almonds, divided
1 cup all-purpose flour
⅓ cup margarine, melted
½ cup sugar, divided
1 package (8 ounces) light cream cheese,
   softened
1 egg
1 teaspoon vanilla extract
1 can (20 ounces) DOLE® Crushed Pineapple in
   Syrup, drained°
⅓ cup flaked coconut

- Chop ¼ cup almonds for crust; mix with flour, margarine and ¼ cup sugar in medium bowl until crumbly. Press into bottom of 9-inch square pan. Bake in 350°F oven 12 minutes.

- Beat cream cheese, egg, remaining ¼ cup sugar, vanilla and pineapple in large bowl until blended. Pour over crust. Top with coconut and remaining ¼ cup sliced almonds.

- Bake in 350°F oven 35 to 40 minutes until golden brown. Cool on wire rack. Refrigerate at least 2 hours before cutting into bars.

°*Use pineapple packed in juice, if desired.*

Nutrients per cookie:

Calories	199	Sodium	111 mg
Fat	10 g	Cholesterol	28 mg

Tropical Bar Cookies

Forgotten Chips Cookies

Under 100 Calories

Makes 2½ dozen cookies

2 egg whites
⅛ teaspoon cream of tartar
⅛ teaspoon salt
⅔ cup sugar
1 teaspoon vanilla extract
1 cup HERSHEY'S® Semi-Sweet Chocolate
    Chips or Milk Chocolate Chips

Heat oven to 375°F. Lightly grease cookie sheets. In small mixer bowl, beat egg whites with cream of tartar and salt until soft peaks form; gradually add sugar, beating until stiff peaks form. Carefully fold in vanilla and chocolate chips. Drop by teaspoonfuls onto prepared cookie sheets. Place cookie sheets in preheated oven; immediately turn off oven and allow cookies to remain 6 hours or overnight, without opening oven door. Remove cookies from cookie sheets. Store in airtight container in cool, dry place.

Nutrients per cookie:			
Calories	98	Sodium	28 mg
Fat	4 g	Cholesterol	0 mg

Peanut Butter Cookies

Under 100 Calories

Makes 4 dozen cookies

⅔ cup firmly packed light brown sugar
½ cup chunky or smooth peanut butter
⅓ cup BLUE BONNET® Margarine, softened
1 egg
½ cup Regular, Instant or Quick CREAM OF
    WHEAT® Cereal, uncooked
1 teaspoon vanilla extract
1¼ cups all-purpose flour
½ teaspoon baking soda

In medium bowl, with electric mixer at medium speed, beat brown sugar, peanut butter, margarine and egg until fluffy; blend in cereal and vanilla. Stir in flour and baking soda to make a stiff dough. Roll dough into 1-inch balls; place 2 inches apart on greased baking sheets. Flatten balls with bottom of floured glass; press with fork tines to make crisscross pattern. Bake at 350°F for 8 to 9 minutes or until lightly browned. Remove from baking sheets; cool on wire racks.

Nutrients per cookie:			
Calories	59	Sodium°	34 mg
Fat	3 g	Cholesterol	4 mg

°*If Using Quick CREAM OF WHEAT®, sodium is 40 mg.*

Cocoa Banana Bars

Low Cholesterol

Makes 9 bars

⅔ cup QUAKER® Oat Bran hot cereal, uncooked
⅔ cup all-purpose flour
½ cup granulated sugar
⅓ cup unsweetened cocoa
½ cup mashed ripe banana (about 1 large)
¼ cup liquid vegetable oil margarine
3 tablespoons light corn syrup
2 egg whites, slightly beaten
1 teaspoon vanilla
2 teaspoons cocoa
2 teaspoons liquid vegetable oil margarine
¼ cup powdered sugar
2 to 2½ teaspoons warm water, divided
    Strawberry halves (optional)

Heat oven to 350°F. Lightly spray 8-inch square baking pan with no-stick cooking spray or oil lightly. Combine oat bran, flour, granulated sugar and ⅓ cup cocoa. Add combined banana, ¼ cup margarine, corn syrup, egg whites and vanilla; mix well. Pour into prepared pan, spreading evenly. Bake 23 to 25 minutes or until center is set. Cool on wire rack; cut into bars. Store tightly covered.

Combine 2 teaspoons cocoa and 2 teaspoons margarine. Stir in powdered sugar and 1 teaspoon of the water. Gradually add remaining 1 to 1½ teaspoons water to make medium-thick glaze, mixing well. Drizzle glaze over brownies. Top with strawberry halves, if desired.

Microwave Directions: Combine oat bran, flour, granulated sugar and ⅓ cup cocoa. Add combined banana, ¼ cup margarine, corn syrup, egg whites and vanilla; mix well. Pour into 9-inch microwavable pie plate, spreading evenly. Place in microwave on inverted microwavable plate. Microwave at HIGH 4 minutes 30 seconds to 5 minutes or until edges are firm to the touch, rotating every 2 minutes. To test for doneness, the surface is firm to the touch and the center may appear slightly wet and soft. Cool; cut into wedges. Store tightly covered. Drizzle with glaze as directed above.

Nutrients per cookie:			
Calories	210	Sodium	60 mg
Fat	7 g	Cholesterol	0 mg

Cocoa Banana Bars

Layered Fruit Bars

Makes 20 bars

Base and Topping
⅓ cup CRISCO® Shortening
½ cup firmly packed brown sugar
¼ teaspoon vanilla extract
1 cup all-purpose flour
⅛ teaspoon salt (optional)
2 teaspoons skim milk
¼ cup quick oats (not instant or old-fashioned), uncooked

Filling
1 cup apricot preserves

Drizzle
¾ cup confectioners sugar
1 tablespoon plus ½ teaspoon skim milk
¼ teaspoon vanilla extract

1. Preheat oven to 375°F.

2. **For Base,** cream Crisco®, brown sugar and vanilla in large bowl at medium speed of electric mixer. Mix in flour, salt (if used) and milk. Reserve ¼ cup mixture for topping. Press remaining mixture evenly in bottom of ungreased 8-inch square pan. Bake at 375°F for 10 minutes or until lightly browned.

3. **For Topping,** combine reserved ¼ cup mixture with oats until crumbly.

4. **For Filling,** spread preserves over hot baked base. Sprinkle with topping. Bake at 375°F for 15 minutes or until top is lightly browned. Cool completely.

5. **For Drizzle,** combine confectioners sugar, milk and vanilla. Drizzle over top. Allow to set before cutting into bars.

Nutrients per bar cookie:

Calories	132	Sodium	18 mg
Fat	3 g	Cholesterol	0 mg

Chocolate Refrigerator Cookies

Makes 4 dozen cookies

1⅔ cups all-purpose flour
⅓ cup NESTLÉ® Cocoa
½ teaspoon baking powder
½ teaspoon cinnamon
¾ cup sugar
½ cup (1 stick) margarine, softened
1 tablespoon skim milk
1 egg
¾ cup ground walnuts

In small bowl, combine flour, cocoa, baking powder and cinnamon; set aside.

In large mixer bowl, beat sugar and margarine until creamy. Beat in milk and egg. Gradually beat in flour mixture. Stir in walnuts. On waxed paper, shape dough into 1½-inch diameter log; roll in waxed paper. Refrigerate 2 to 3 hours or overnight.

Preheat oven to 350°F. Cut log into ¼-inch slices. Place on ungreased cookie sheets. Bake 10 minutes. Let stand on cookie sheets 2 minutes. Remove from cookie sheets; cool.

Nutrients per cookie:

Calories	56	Sodium	27 mg
Fat	3 g	Cholesterol	4 mg

Cranberry-Orange Muesli Bars

Makes 24 bars

Filling
1 package (12 ounces) cranberries, fresh or frozen
1 cup granulated sugar
1 teaspoon grated orange peel, optional
1 cup orange juice

Base and Topping
4 cups RALSTON® Brand Fruit & Nut Muesli cereal, crushed to 3 cups
1½ cups all-purpose flour
¾ cup packed brown sugar
1½ teaspoons baking powder
½ teaspoon salt
¾ cup (1½ sticks) margarine or butter, softened

To prepare Filling: In medium saucepan over medium heat combine cranberries, granulated sugar, orange peel and orange juice. Cook, stirring frequently, until mixture comes to a boil; reduce heat and simmer 15 to 18 minutes, stirring frequently. Cool.

To prepare Base and Topping: Preheat oven to 350°. In large bowl combine cereal, flour, brown sugar, baking powder and salt. Mix in margarine until crumbly. Reserve 1½ cups mixture for topping; set aside. Press remaining cereal mixture firmly and evenly into ungreased 13×9×2-inch baking pan. Bake 10 minutes. Spread cranberry filling evenly over base; sprinkle with reserved 1½ cups cereal mixture. Bake an additional 18 to 20 minutes or until lightly browned.

Nutrients per 2-inch bar:

Calories	199	Sodium	167 mg
Fat	7 g	Cholesterol	0 mg

Apricot-Pecan Tassies

Apricot-Pecan Tassies

Under 200 Calories

Makes 24 cookies

1 cup all-purpose flour
½ cup butter, cut into pieces
6 tablespoons light cream cheese
¾ cup light brown sugar, firmly packed
1 egg, lightly beaten
1 tablespoon butter, softened
½ teaspoon vanilla extract
¼ teaspoon salt
⅔ cup Dried California Apricot Halves, diced
    (about 4 ounces)
⅓ cup chopped pecans

In food processor, combine flour, ½ cup butter and cream cheese; process until mixture forms a ball. Wrap dough in plastic wrap and chill 15 minutes. Meanwhile, prepare filling by combining brown sugar, egg, 1 tablespoon butter, vanilla and salt in medium bowl; beat until smooth. Stir in apricots and nuts. Preheat oven to 325°F. Shape dough into 24 (1-inch) balls and place in paper-lined or greased (1½-inch) miniature muffin cups or tart pans. Press dough on bottom and sides of each cup; fill with 1 teaspoon apricot-pecan filling. Bake 25 minutes or until golden and filling sets. Cool slightly and remove from cups. Cookies can be wrapped tightly in plastic and frozen for up to 6 weeks.

Nutrients per cookie:

Calories	110	Sodium	85 mg
Fat	7 g	Cholesterol	13 mg

Favorite recipe from **California Apricot Advisory Board**.

Chocolate Chip Raspberry Jumbles

Chocolate Chip Raspberry Jumbles

Makes 16 bars

1 package DUNCAN HINES® Chocolate Chip
   Cookie Mix
½ cup seedless red raspberry preserves

1. Preheat oven to 350°F.

2. Prepare chocolate chip cookie mix following package directions. Reserve ½ cup dough.

3. Spread remaining dough into ungreased 9-inch square pan. Spread preserves over base. Drop teaspoonfuls of reserved dough randomly over top. Bake at 350°F for 20 to 25 minutes or until golden brown.

Nutrients per cookie:

Calories	178	Sodium	95 mg
Fat	6 g	Cholesterol	13 mg

Mocha Cookies

Under 100 Calories

Makes 40 cookies

2½ tablespoons instant coffee
1½ tablespoons skim milk
⅓ cup light brown sugar
¼ cup granulated sugar
¼ cup margarine
1 egg
½ teaspoon almond extract
2 cups all-purpose flour, sifted
¼ cup wheat flakes cereal
¼ teaspoon baking powder
½ teaspoon cinnamon

Preheat oven to 350°F. Spray cookie sheets with non-stick cooking spray. In small cup, dissolve coffee in milk. In large bowl, cream together sugars and margarine. Beat in egg, almond extract and coffee mixture. Stir together flour, wheat flakes, baking powder and cinnamon; beat into sugar mixture gradually. Drop by teaspoonfuls, 2 inches apart, onto cookie sheets. Flatten with back of fork. Bake 8 to 10 minutes or until set. Remove from cookie sheets. Cool completely.

Nutrients per cookie:

Calories	44	Sodium	21 mg
Fat	1 g	Cholesterol	5 mg

Favorite recipe from **The Sugar Association.**

Giant Raisin Bran Cookies

Under 200 Calories

Makes 18 cookies

2 cups KELLOGG'S® RAISIN BRAN cereal,
   crushed to 1½ cups
1 cup whole wheat flour
1 cup all-purpose flour
1 teaspoon baking soda
¾ cup margarine, softened
⅔ cup granulated sugar
½ cup firmly packed brown sugar
2 eggs

1. Stir together Kellogg's® Raisin Bran cereal, flours and soda; set aside.

2. In large mixing bowl, beat margarine and sugars until light and fluffy. Add eggs; beat well. Stir in cereal mixture, thoroughly combining. Drop by scant ¼ cup measure 4 inches apart onto ungreased cookie sheet.

3. Bake in 350°F oven about 14 minutes or until lightly browned. Cool 1 minute on cookie sheet. Cool completely on wire rack.

Nutrients per cookie:

Calories	190	Sodium	183 mg
Fat	9 g	Cholesterol	24 mg

Chocolate Candy Cookies

Under 100 Calories

Makes 4½ dozen cookies

⅔ cup MIRACLE WHIP® Salad Dressing
1 two-layer devil's food cake mix
2 eggs
1 (8 oz.) pkg. multicolored milk chocolate candies

• Preheat oven to 375°.

• Blend salad dressing, cake mix and eggs at low speed with electric mixer until moistened. Beat on medium speed 2 minutes. Stir in candies. (Dough will be stiff.)

• Drop rounded teaspoonfuls of dough, 2 inches apart, onto greased cookie sheets.

• Bake 9 to 11 minutes or until almost set. (Cookies will still appear soft.) Cool 1 minute; remove from cookie sheets.

Nutrients per cookie:

Calories	80	Sodium	95 mg
Fat	3 g	Cholesterol	10 mg

Raisin, Oat & Almond Bars

Low Cholesterol

Makes 20 bars

2 cups QUAKER® Oats (Quick or Old Fashioned, uncooked)
1½ cups all-purpose flour
¾ cup firmly packed brown sugar
½ teaspoon baking soda
¼ teaspoon grated lemon peel
¼ teaspoon ground cinnamon
¾ cup (1½ sticks) margarine, melted
1½ cups raisins
⅔ cup water
2 tablespoons granulated sugar
2 teaspoons cornstarch
⅓ cup sliced almonds

Heat oven to 350°F. Lightly spray 13×9-inch baking pan with no-stick cooking spray or oil lightly. Combine oats, flour, brown sugar, baking soda, lemon peel and cinnamon. Add margarine, mixing until crumbly. Reserve 1 cup for topping; press remaining mixture onto bottom of prepared pan. Bake 15 minutes.

In small saucepan, combine remaining ingredients except almonds; bring to a boil, stirring frequently. Reduce heat; simmer 30 seconds to 1 minute or until thickened and clear, stirring constantly. Cool slightly. Pour over crust. Sprinkle with reserved 1 cup oat topping and almonds. Bake 20 to 25 minutes or until edges are lightly browned. Cool; cut into bars. Store loosely covered in cool place.

Microwave Directions: Prepare crust and topping as directed above. For raisin filling, combine raisins, water, granulated sugar and cornstarch in 1-qt. microwavable measuring cup or bowl. Microwave at HIGH 2 minutes; stir. Microwave an additional 1 minute 30 seconds to 2 minutes or until thickened and clear, stirring every minute. Cool slightly. Proceed as above.

Nutrients per bar:

Calories	210	Sodium	110 mg
Fat	8 g	Cholesterol	0 mg

Chocolate Fruit Crispies

Under 100 Calories

Makes 8 dozen crispies

6 cups crisp rice cereal
½ cup raisins
½ cup finely chopped dried apricots
1 bag (10 ounces) large marshmallows (about 40)
½ cup (3 ounces) semisweet chocolate morsels
2 tablespoons milk
Vegetable cooking spray

Combine cereal, raisins, and apricots in large bowl; set aside. Combine marshmallows, chocolate, and milk in 2-quart saucepan. Place over low heat and cook, stirring, about 10 minutes or until melted. Pour over cereal mixture; mix well. Coat 12×8×2-inch baking pan with cooking spray; spread mixture evenly into pan. Press down firmly using fingers coated with cooking spray. Cover and chill until firm. Cut into 1-inch squares.

To microwave: Combine cereal, raisins, and apricots in large bowl; set aside. Combine marshmallows, chocolate, and milk in 1½-quart microproof dish. Cook, uncovered, on HIGH 1 minute; stir until smooth. Continue as directed above.

Nutrients per cookie:

Calories	25	Sodium	24 mg
Fat	0 g	Cholesterol	0 mg

Favorite recipe from **USA Rice Council.**

Painted Desert Brownies

Under 200 Calories

Makes 40 brownies

3 cups RICE CHEX® brand cereal, crushed to 1 cup
1 cup all-purpose flour
¾ cup granulated sugar
½ teaspoon baking powder
½ cup margarine or butter, melted
4 teaspoons instant coffee, dissolved in 2 teaspoons boiling water, divided
1 package (21.5 ounces) chocolate brownie mix
1 package (8 ounces) cream cheese
1 egg, beaten
¼ cup powdered sugar

Preheat oven to 350°. In large bowl combine cereal, flour, granulated sugar and baking powder. Add margarine and 1 teaspoon of the coffee mixture, stirring until well combined. Press evenly and firmly into ungreased 13×9×2-inch baking pan. Bake 10 minutes. Meanwhile prepare brownie mix according to package directions but do not bake; set aside. In medium bowl, beat cream cheese, egg, powdered sugar and remaining 1 teaspoon coffee mixture until well combined. Pour reserved brownie mixture over hot crust. Spoon cream cheese mixture in several places over brownie mixture. Swirl cream cheese mixture into brownie mixture with knife. Bake 30 to 35 minutes or until set. Cool. Cut into squares.

Nutrients per brownie:

Calories	145	Sodium	120 mg
Fat	6 g	Cholesterol	20 mg

Chocolate Biscotti

Makes 4 dozen cookies

1½ cups all-purpose flour
½ cup NESTLÉ® Cocoa
1½ teaspoons baking powder
½ teaspoon baking soda
⅔ cup sugar
3 tablespoons butter, softened
2 eggs
½ teaspoon almond extract
½ cup almonds, coarsely chopped

Preheat oven to 350°F. Grease 15½×10½×1-inch baking pan. In small bowl, combine flour, cocoa, baking powder and baking soda; set aside.

In large mixer bowl, beat sugar, butter, eggs and almond extract until creamy. Gradually beat in flour mixture. Stir in almonds. Divide dough in half. Shape into two 12-inch long logs; flatten slightly. Place in prepared pan.

Bake 25 minutes. Cool in pan on wire rack 5 minutes. Cut into ½-inch thick slices; return slices to pan, cut-sides down. Bake 20 minutes longer. Cool completely.

Nutrients per cookie:			
Calories	46	Sodium	29 mg
Fat	2 g	Cholesterol	11 mg

Orange Sugar Cookies

Makes 3½ dozen cookies

2 cups all-purpose flour
1½ teaspoons baking soda
1 cup sugar
½ cup FLEISCHMANN'S® Margarine, softened
2 teaspoons grated orange peel
1 teaspoon vanilla extract
¼ cup EGG BEATERS® 99% Real Egg Product
Sugar, optional

In small bowl, combine flour and baking soda; set aside.

In medium bowl, with electric mixer at medium speed, beat sugar, margarine, orange peel and vanilla until creamy. Add Egg Beaters®; beat 1 minute. Gradually stir in flour mixture until blended. Chill dough 1 hour.

Shape dough into 42 (¾-inch) balls; roll in sugar. Place 2 inches apart on lightly greased baking sheets. Bake at 375°F for 8 to 10 minutes or until light golden brown. Remove from baking sheets. Cool on wire racks.

Nutrients per cookie:			
Calories	60	Sodium	49 mg
Fat	2 g	Cholesterol	0 mg

Chocolate Biscotti

Banana Cookies

Under 200 Calories

Makes 4 dozen cookies

  2 ripe, medium DOLE® Bananas, peeled
1½ cups all-purpose flour
  ½ teaspoon baking soda
  ½ teaspoon salt
  ½ teaspoon ground cinnamon
  ¼ teaspoon ground nutmeg
1½ cups brown sugar, packed
  ¾ cup margarine, softened
  1 egg
  ½ cup light dairy sour cream
  1 teaspoon vanilla extract
1½ cups rolled oats
  1 cup DOLE® Golden Raisins
  ¾ cup DOLE® Chopped Almonds, toasted

- Place bananas in blender. Process until puréed; use 1 cup for recipe.
- Combine flour, baking soda, salt and spices in small bowl.
- Beat brown sugar and margarine in large bowl until light and fluffy. Beat in 1 cup bananas, egg, sour cream and vanilla.
- Beat in flour mixture until well blended. Stir in oats, raisins and almonds. Cover and refrigerate dough 1 hour to firm.
- Drop batter by heaping tablespoonfuls onto greased cookie sheets 2 inches apart.
- Bake in 350°F oven 15 to 20 minutes or until cookies are slightly brown around edges. Cool on wire racks.

Nutrients per cookie:

Calories	113	Sodium	72 mg
Fat	5 g	Cholesterol	7 mg

Banana Cookies

Crunchy Fruit Bars

Low Cholesterol

Makes 12 bars

1½ cups KRETSCHMER® Original or Honey Crunch Wheat Germ
  ¾ cup all-purpose flour
  ½ cup firmly packed brown sugar
  ½ cup chopped pecans
  ⅓ cup margarine, melted
  2 egg whites, slightly beaten
  ½ teaspoon ground cinnamon
  ¾ cup preserves, any flavor

Heat oven to 375°F. Lightly spray 8- or 9-inch square baking pan with no-stick cooking spray. Combine all ingredients except preserves. Reserve ½ cup mixture; firmly press remaining mixture onto bottom of prepared pan. Spread preserves evenly over base; sprinkle with reserved ½ cup mixture. Bake 20 to 25 minutes or until preserves are bubbly and topping is golden brown. Cool; cut into bars. Store loosely covered.

Nutrients per bar:

Calories	250	Sodium	75 mg
Fat	10 g	Cholesterol	0 mg

Cholesterol-Free Chocolate Oatmeal Cookies

Under 200 Calories

Makes 2 dozen cookies

2¼ cups quick oats, uncooked
  1 cup all-purpose flour
  ½ teaspoon baking soda
  ½ teaspoon cinnamon
  ¾ cup sugar
  ½ cup (1 stick) margarine, softened
  2 egg whites
  1 teaspoon vanilla extract
One 6-oz. pkg. (1 cup) NESTLÉ® TOLL HOUSE® Semi-Sweet Chocolate Morsels

Preheat oven to 350°F. In small bowl, combine oats, flour, baking soda and cinnamon; set aside.

In large mixer bowl, beat sugar, margarine, egg whites and vanilla extract until creamy. Gradually stir in flour mixture and semi-sweet chocolate morsels. Drop by rounded tablespoonfuls onto ungreased cookie sheets.

Bake 12 to 15 minutes. Let stand on cookie sheets 2 minutes. Remove from cookie sheets; cool.

Nutrients per cookie:

Calories	144	Sodium	66 mg
Fat	6 g	Cholesterol	0 mg

Baked Truffle Treasures

Makes 30 cookies

1 cup granulated sugar
¼ cup (½ stick) butter, melted
2 eggs, beaten
3 tablespoons cherry brandy or amaretto *or*
    ½ teaspoon almond extract
2 tablespoons honey
1 teaspoon vanilla extract
2 cups ALMOND DELIGHT® brand cereal,
    crushed to 1 cup
½ cup unsweetened cocoa
½ cup flaked coconut
½ cup powdered sugar

Preheat oven to 350°. In medium bowl, beat granulated sugar and butter. Add eggs, brandy, honey and vanilla, stirring until well combined. Stir in cereal, cocoa and coconut. Pour into ungreased 2-quart casserole. Bake 30 minutes. Remove from oven and stir immediately until well blended. Let cool to room temperature. Shape level tablespoons of mixture into 1½-inch balls. Roll each ball in powdered sugar. Store in airtight container.

Microwave Directions: Follow directions above for combining ingredients. Pour batter into ungreased microwave-safe 2-quart casserole dish. Microwave on HIGH 5 to 6 minutes, turning dish ¼-turn halfway through. Remove from microwave and stir immediately until well blended. Let cool to room temperature. Shape as directed above.

Nutrients per cookie:			
Calories	78	Sodium	39 mg
Fat	3 g	Cholesterol	18 mg

Cranberry Thumbprints

Makes 2 dozen cookies

1 cup OCEAN SPRAY® Cran-Fruit™ Sauce
1 package (20 ounces) refrigerated sugar cookie
    dough
½ cup powdered sugar
1 tablespoon water

Preheat oven to 350°F. Drain Cran-Fruit™. Roll dough to form 24 (1-inch) balls. Place on cookie sheets; press thumb into center of each ball. Place scant 1 teaspoon Cran-Fruit™ in the indent of each cookie. Bake 7 to 11 minutes or until lightly browned. Cool slightly before transferring to wire rack. Combine powdered sugar and water; drizzle glaze onto each cookie.

Nutrients per cookie:			
Calories	145	Sodium	131 mg
Fat	6 g	Cholesterol	14 mg

Peanut Butter Bars

Peanut Butter Bars

Makes 24 bars

1 package DUNCAN HINES® Peanut Butter
    Cookie Mix
2 egg whites
½ cup chopped peanuts
1 cup confectioners sugar
2 tablespoons water
½ teaspoon vanilla extract

1. Preheat oven to 350°F.

2. Combine cookie mix, peanut butter packet from Mix and egg whites in large bowl. Stir until thoroughly blended. Press in ungreased 13×9×2-inch pan. Sprinkle peanuts over dough. Press lightly. Bake at 350°F for 16 to 18 minutes or until golden brown. Cool completely. Combine confectioners sugar, water and vanilla extract in small bowl. Stir until blended. Drizzle glaze over top. Cut into bars.

Nutrients per cookie:			
Calories	65	Sodium	104 mg
Fat	7 g	Cholesterol	0 mg

Nutty Blueberry Muffins

Bread Basket
◆◇◆
TREATS

Nutty Blueberry Muffins

Low Cholesterol

Makes 8 large or 12 medium muffins

1 package DUNCAN HINES® Blueberry
    Muffin Mix
2 egg whites
½ cup water
⅓ cup chopped pecans

1. Preheat oven to 400°F. Grease 2½-inch muffin cups (or use paper liners).

2. Rinse blueberries from Mix with cold water and drain.

3. Empty muffin mix into bowl. Break up any lumps. Add egg whites and water. Stir until moistened, about 50 strokes. Stir in nuts; fold in blueberries.

4. For large muffins, fill cups ⅔ full. Bake at 400°F for 17 to 22 minutes or until toothpick inserted in center comes out clean. For medium muffins, fill cups ½ full. Bake at 400°F for 15 to 20 minutes. Cool 5 to 10 minutes.

Nutrients per muffin (for 8 large):			
Calories	202	Sodium	284 mg
Fat	6 g	Cholesterol	0 mg

Nutrients per muffin (for 12 medium):			
Calories	135	Sodium	189 mg
Fat	4 g	Cholesterol	0 mg

Cocoa Banana-Nut Bread

Low Cholesterol

Makes 1 loaf, 16 servings

2 extra-ripe, medium DOLE® Bananas, peeled
1½ cups all-purpose flour
1⅓ cups sugar
6 tablespoons unsweetened cocoa
1 teaspoon baking soda
½ teaspoon salt
¼ teaspoon baking powder
2 eggs
½ cup vegetable oil
⅓ cup DOLE® Chopped Almonds

• Place bananas in blender. Process until puréed; use 1 cup for recipe.

• Combine flour, sugar, cocoa, baking soda, salt and baking powder in large bowl. Add eggs, oil and 1 cup banana; beat just until all ingredients are well blended. Stir in almonds.

• Pour batter into greased 9×5-inch loaf pan. Bake in 350°F oven 55 to 60 minutes or until cake tester inserted in center comes out clean. Cool in pan on wire rack 10 minutes. Remove from pan. Cool completely on wire rack before slicing. Loaf may be stored in refrigerator, well wrapped, for 1 week.

Nutrients per serving (1 slice):			
Calories	218	Sodium	154 mg
Fat	10 g	Cholesterol	34 mg

Time-Saver Coffeecake

Low Cholesterol

Makes 9 servings

Topping
- 1 cup KELLOGG'S® COMMON SENSE™ Oat Bran cereal, any variety
- ⅓ cup firmly packed brown sugar
- ½ teaspoon ground cinnamon
- 2 tablespoons margarine, softened

Coffeecake
- 1½ cups KELLOGG'S® COMMON SENSE™ Oat Bran cereal, any variety
- 1 cup all-purpose flour
- ½ cup granulated sugar
- 1 teaspoon baking powder
- ½ teaspoon ground cinnamon
- ¼ teaspoon salt
- ½ cup buttermilk
- ¼ cup margarine, softened
- 2 egg whites

1. **For Topping,** combine topping ingredients in small bowl, mixing until evenly combined; set aside.

2. **For Coffeecake,** in large mixing bowl, combine 1½ cups Kellogg's® Common Sense™ Oat Bran cereal, flour, granulated sugar, baking powder, cinnamon and salt. Stir in buttermilk, ¼ cup margarine and egg whites, beating until thoroughly combined. Spread batter evenly in greased 8-inch square baking pan. Sprinkle reserved cereal topping over batter. Cover pan tightly with foil. Refrigerate overnight or bake immediately.

3. Bake covered in 350°F oven about 30 minutes or until lightly browned and wooden pick inserted near center comes out clean. Cut into squares. Serve warm.

Nutrients per serving:

Calories	260	Sodium	269 mg
Fat	8 g	Cholesterol	0 mg

Lemon Yogurt-Raisin Tea Bread

Under 200 Calories

Makes 12 slices

- 1¼ cups all-purpose flour
- ¾ cup whole-wheat flour
- 4 tablespoons granulated sugar, divided
- 2 teaspoons baking powder
- ½ teaspoon baking soda
- ¼ teaspoon salt
- 1½ cups DANNON® Lemon Lowfat Yogurt
- ¼ cup unsalted butter or margarine, melted and cooled slightly
- 1 large egg
- ¾ cup raisins

Heat oven to 350°. Grease 8½×4½×2½-inch loaf pan. Mix flours, 3 tablespoons of the sugar, baking powder, baking soda and salt in large bowl. Measure yogurt in 1-quart glass measure. Add butter and egg and beat with fork until well blended. Pour yogurt mixture into dry ingredients. Add raisins and stir just until dry ingredients are moistened. Pour into prepared pan. Smooth batter with spatula. Sprinkle with remaining 1 tablespoon sugar. Bake 40 to 45 minutes, until bread is lightly browned, springy to the touch and a toothpick inserted just off center comes out clean. Cool on wire rack 30 minutes. Turn out of pan; invert so sugared side is up. Cool completely before serving.

Nutrients per serving:

Calories	185	Sodium	165 mg
Fat	5 g	Cholesterol	35 mg

Fresh Apple Muffins

Under 200 Calories

Makes 1 dozen muffins

- 3 NABISCO® Shredded Wheat biscuits or 1½ cups SPOON SIZE® Shredded Wheat, finely rolled
- 1¼ cups all-purpose flour
- ¼ cup firmly packed light brown sugar
- 1 tablespoon DAVIS® Baking Powder
- ½ teaspoon ground cinnamon
- ¾ cup chopped peeled baking apple (about 1 medium)
- ⅔ cup skim milk
- ¼ cup FLEISCHMANN'S® Margarine, melted
- ¼ cup EGG BEATERS® 99% Real Egg Product

In medium bowl, combine cereal, flour, brown sugar, baking powder and cinnamon. In another bowl, blend apple, milk, margarine and Egg Beaters®; stir into flour mixture just until blended.

Spoon batter into 12 greased 2½-inch muffin-pan cups. Bake at 400°F for 25 minutes or until toothpick inserted in center comes out clean. Remove from pan. Cool slightly.

Nutrients per muffin:

Calories	132	Sodium	154 mg
Fat	4 g	Cholesterol	0 mg

Peachy Cinnamon Coffeecake

Peachy Cinnamon Coffeecake

Low Cholesterol

9 servings

1 package DUNCAN HINES® Bakery Style
    Cinnamon Swirl Muffin Mix
1 can (8¼ ounces) juice pack sliced yellow cling
    peaches
1 egg

1. Preheat oven to 400°F. Grease 8-inch square or
9-inch round pan.

2. Drain peaches, reserving juice. *Add water to
reserved juice to equal ¾ cup liquid.* Chop peaches.

3. Combine muffin mix, egg and ¾ cup peach liquid
in medium bowl; fold in peaches. Pour batter into
pan. Knead swirl packet from Mix 10 seconds before
opening. Squeeze contents on top of batter and swirl
with knife. Sprinkle topping from Mix over batter.
Bake at 400°F for 28 to 33 minutes for 8-inch pan (or
20 to 25 minutes for 9-inch pan) or until golden.
Serve warm.

Nutrients per serving:

Calories	273	Sodium	328 mg
Fat	9 g	Cholesterol	24 mg

Orange Blossom Muffins

Low Cholesterol

Makes 12 large muffins

1 package DUNCAN HINES® Bakery Style
    Pecan Crunch Muffin Mix
½ teaspoon baking powder
2 egg whites
¾ cup CITRUS HILL® Orange Juice
½ cup orange marmalade

1. Preheat oven to 400°F. Grease top surface of
12-cup muffin pan. Line with 2½-inch foil or paper
liners.

2. Empty muffin mix into medium bowl. Add baking
powder; stir to combine and break up any lumps. Add
egg whites and orange juice. Stir until moistened,
about 50 strokes. Fold in marmalade. Fill muffin cups
two-thirds full. Sprinkle with topping from Mix. Bake
at 400°F for 18 to 20 minutes or until toothpick
inserted in center comes out clean. Cool 5 to 10
minutes. Loosen muffins carefully before removing
from pan. Serve warm.

Nutrients per muffin:

Calories	255	Sodium	271 mg
Fat	10 g	Cholesterol	0 mg

Lemon Glazed Peach Muffins

Makes 8 muffins

1 cup all-purpose flour
3 tablespoons sugar
2 teaspoons baking powder
½ teaspoon salt
½ teaspoon pumpkin pie spice
1 can (16 ounces) sliced cling peaches in light syrup
1 cup KELLOGG'S® ALL-BRAN® cereal
½ cup skim milk
1 egg white
2 tablespoons vegetable oil
Lemon Sauce (recipe follows)

1. Stir together flour, sugar, baking powder, salt and pumpkin pie spice. Set aside.

2. Drain peaches reserving ⅓ cup syrup. Set aside 8 peach slices; chop remaining peach slices.

3. Measure Kellogg's® All-Bran® cereal, milk and the ⅓ cup syrup into large mixing bowl. Stir to combine. Let stand 2 minutes or until cereal is softened. Add egg white and oil. Beat well. Stir in chopped peaches.

4. Add flour mixture, stirring only until combined. Portion batter evenly into 8 lightly greased 2½-inch muffin-pan cups. Place 1 peach slice over top of each muffin.

5. Bake at 400°F about 25 minutes or until golden brown. Serve warm with Lemon Sauce.

Lemon Sauce

⅓ cup sugar
2 tablespoons cornstarch
1½ cups cold water
1 teaspoon grated lemon peel
1 tablespoon lemon juice

Combine sugar and cornstarch in 2-quart saucepan. Add water, stirring until smooth. Cook over medium heat, stirring constantly, until mixture boils. Continue cooking and stirring 3 minutes longer. Remove from heat; stir in lemon peel and juice. Serve hot over warm Peach Muffins.

Nutrients per serving (1 muffin plus 3 tablespoons sauce):			
Calories	210	Sodium	355 mg
Fat	4 g	Cholesterol	1 mg

Orange Chocolate Chip Bread

Makes 16 servings

1 cup skim milk
¼ cup orange juice
⅓ cup sugar
1 egg, slightly beaten
1 tablespoon freshly grated orange peel
3 cups all-purpose biscuit baking mix
½ cup HERSHEY'S® MINI CHIPS Semi-Sweet Chocolate

Heat oven to 350°F. Grease 9×5×3-inch loaf pan. In medium bowl, combine milk, orange juice, sugar, egg and orange peel; stir in baking mix. Beat with spoon until well combined, about 1 minute. Stir in Mini Chips. Pour batter into prepared pan. Bake about 45 to 50 minutes or until wooden pick inserted in center comes out clean. Cool 10 minutes; remove from pan to wire rack. Cool completely. Slice and serve. To store leftovers, wrap in foil or plastic wrap.

Nutrients per serving:			
Calories	161	Sodium	274 mg
Fat	5 g	Cholesterol	17 mg

Cinnamon Apple-Nut Muffins

Makes 1 dozen muffins

¾ cup peeled, finely chopped apple
½ cup sugar, divided
1 teaspoon ground cinnamon
1 cup all-purpose flour
¾ cup whole wheat flour
2 teaspoons baking powder
¼ teaspoon salt
1 cup low-fat (1%) milk
2 tablespoons margarine, melted
2 egg whites, lightly beaten
¼ cup chopped walnuts
Sugar, for topping (optional)

Preheat oven to 400°F. In small bowl, toss apple with ¼ cup of the sugar and the cinnamon. In large bowl, combine remaining ¼ cup sugar, the flours, baking powder and salt. Mix together milk, melted margarine and egg whites; stir into dry ingredients just until moistened. Add apple and nuts. Fill lightly greased muffin cups ¾ full; sprinkle each lightly with sugar, if desired. Bake 20 to 25 minutes or until toothpick inserted in center comes out clean.

Nutrients per muffin:			
Calories	114	Sodium	177 mg
Fat	4 g	Cholesterol	24 mg

Favorite recipe from **The Sugar Association**.

Apple Bran Loaf

Makes 1 loaf

1½ cups all-purpose flour
½ cup sugar
1 teaspoon baking powder
1 teaspoon baking soda
1 teaspoon ground cinnamon
1½ cups NABISCO® 100% Bran™
1 cup seedless raisins
¼ cup margarine, melted
⅔ cup hot water
1 cup MOTT'S® Regular Apple Sauce
1 egg, slightly beaten
1 teaspoon vanilla extract

In medium bowl, mix flour, sugar, baking powder, baking soda and cinnamon; set aside. In separate bowl, mix bran, raisins, margarine and hot water; let stand 5 minutes. Add apple sauce, egg and vanilla. With mixer at medium speed, beat for 2 minutes. Stir in flour mixture just until blended. Spread in greased 9×5×3-inch loaf pan. Bake at 350°F for 55 minutes or until toothpick inserted in center comes out clean. Cool in pan 10 minutes. Remove from pan; cool on wire rack.

Nutrients per ½-inch-thick slice:

Calories	157	Sodium	161 mg
Fat	4 g	Cholesterol	13 mg

Carrot Raisin Coffee Cake

Makes 12 servings

⅓ cup margarine, melted
⅓ cup firmly packed brown sugar
2 eggs
1 teaspoon vanilla
1½ cups QUAKER® Oats (Quick or Old Fashioned, uncooked)
¾ cup all-purpose flour
1 teaspoon ground cinnamon
¾ teaspoon baking powder
¼ teaspoon baking soda
1 cup shredded carrots
⅓ cup raisins
¼ cup chopped nuts

Heat oven to 375°F. Lightly spray 8-inch square baking pan with no-stick cooking spray or oil lightly. Combine margarine, sugar, eggs and vanilla; mix well. Add oats, flour, cinnamon, baking powder and baking soda; mix well. Stir in carrots, raisins and nuts. Spread into prepared pan; bake 25 to 30 minutes or until wooden pick inserted in center comes out clean.

Nutrients per serving:

Calories	180	Sodium	120 mg
Fat	8 g	Cholesterol	35 mg

Apple Bran Loaf

Cottage Cake Muffins

Cottage Cake Muffins

Under 200 Calories

Makes 20 muffins

2¼ cups all-purpose flour
  2 teaspoons baking powder
  ½ teaspoon baking soda
  1 teaspoon ground cinnamon
  ¼ teaspoon ground nutmeg
  ¼ teaspoon salt
  ½ cup butter or margarine, softened
  ½ cup packed light brown sugar
  ½ cup granulated sugar
  3 eggs
1¾ cups (16-ounce can) LIBBY'S® Solid Pack
     Pumpkin
  ¼ cup milk
  2 teaspoons orange zest
  1 cup chopped assorted dried fruits or raisins
     Quick Drizzle Frosting (recipe follows)

In medium mixing bowl, combine flour, baking powder, baking soda, cinnamon, nutmeg, and salt; set aside. In large mixer bowl, cream butter and sugars. Add eggs; beat until light and fluffy. Blend in pumpkin, milk, and orange zest. Add dry ingredients; mix well. Stir in chopped fruits. Spoon mixture into greased muffin cups, filling ¾ full. Bake in preheated 350°F oven for 25 to 30 minutes, or until toothpick inserted in center comes out clean. Immediately remove from pans; cool on wire racks. Drizzle with Quick Drizzle Frosting.

Quick Drizzle Frosting: In small bowl, combine 1 cup sifted powdered sugar and 2 to 3 tablespoons cream or fresh lemon juice.

Nutrients per muffin:			
Calories	196	Sodium	180 mg
Fat	6 g	Cholesterol	46 mg

Pineapple-Currant Bread

Makes 16 slices

1¾ cups all-purpose flour
½ cup sugar
1½ teaspoons baking powder
¼ teaspoon baking soda
¼ teaspoon salt
3 cups KELLOGG'S® Bran Flakes cereal
1 can (8 ounces) crushed pineapple, drained
¾ cup orange juice
½ cup currants
¼ cup vegetable oil
3 egg whites

1. Stir together flour, sugar, baking powder, baking soda and salt; set aside.

2. In large mixing bowl, beat together Kellogg's® Bran Flakes cereal and remaining ingredients until well mixed. Stir in dry ingredients, mixing until combined. Spread in lightly greased 9×5×3-inch loaf pan.

3. Bake in 350°F oven about 55 minutes or until wooden pick inserted in center comes out clean. Cool 5 minutes before removing from pan. Let cool completely before slicing.

Nutrients per slice:			
Calories	160	Sodium	157 mg
Fat	4 g	Cholesterol	0 mg

Pumpkin-Filled Coffeecake

Makes 12 servings

1 cup plus 3 tablespoons sugar, divided
½ cup (1 stick) margarine, softened, divided
3 egg whites
1 teaspoon vanilla
1 cup skim milk
1¾ cups all-purpose flour
1¾ cups QUAKER® Oats (Quick or Old Fashioned, uncooked), divided
1 tablespoon baking powder
1 cup canned pumpkin
½ teaspoon pumpkin pie spice
⅓ cup KRETSCHMER® Original or Honey Crunch Wheat Germ

Heat oven to 350°F. Spray 13×9-inch baking pan with no-stick cooking spray or oil lightly. Beat 1 cup of the sugar and ⅓ cup of the margarine until fluffy. Add egg whites and vanilla; mix well. Stir in milk and combined flour, 1 cup of the oats and the baking powder. Combine 1 cup batter, pumpkin and spice; set aside. Spread half of remaining batter into pan. Top with pumpkin mixture; spread other half of batter over pumpkin. Melt remaining margarine. Combine with remaining ¾ cup oats, 3 tablespoons sugar and the wheat germ. Sprinkle over batter. Bake 30 to 40 minutes or until golden. Refrigerate leftovers.

Nutrients per serving:			
Calories	290	Sodium	220 mg
Fat	9 g	Cholesterol	0 mg

Butterscotch Apple Muffins

Makes 18 muffins

1⅓ cups whole-wheat flour
1 cup all-purpose flour
1 cup (half of 12-oz. pkg.) NESTLÉ® Toll House® Butterscotch Flavored Morsels
½ cup sugar
4 teaspoons baking powder
½ teaspoon ground cinnamon
¼ teaspoon salt
1½ cups skim milk
6 tablespoons vegetable oil
1 egg
1 apple, chopped

Preheat oven to 400°F. Grease or paper-line 18 muffin cups. In large bowl, combine whole-wheat flour, all-purpose flour, butterscotch morsels, sugar, baking powder, cinnamon and salt. In small bowl, combine milk, oil, egg and apple. Stir into flour mixture just until dry ingredients are moistened. Spoon into prepared muffin cups, filling each ¾ full.

Bake 18 to 20 minutes until wooden toothpick inserted into center comes out clean. (Muffins will be light in color.) Cool 5 minutes; remove from cups. Serve warm or cool completely.

Nutrients per muffin:			
Calories	183	Sodium	128 mg
Fat	8 g	Cholesterol	13 mg

Lemon Cranberry Loaves

Under 200 Calories

Makes 24 slices

1 package DUNCAN HINES® Moist Deluxe
   Lemon Supreme Cake Mix
1¼ cups finely chopped fresh cranberries
½ cup finely chopped walnuts
¼ cup sugar
1 package (3 ounces) cream cheese, softened
¾ cup milk
4 eggs
   Confectioners sugar

1. Preheat oven to 350°F. Grease and flour two 8½×4½-inch loaf pans.

2. Stir together cranberries, walnuts and sugar in medium bowl; set aside.

3. Combine cake mix, cream cheese and milk in large bowl. Beat at medium speed with electric mixer for 2 minutes. Add eggs, one at a time, beating for an additional 2 minutes. Fold in cranberry mixture. Pour into pans. Bake at 350°F for 45 to 50 minutes or until toothpick inserted in center comes out clean. Cool in pan 15 minutes. Loosen loaves from pans. Invert onto cooling rack. Turn right side up. Cool completely. Dust with confectioners sugar.

Nutrients per slice:

Calories	143	Sodium	165 mg
Fat	6 g	Cholesterol	40 mg

Oatmeal Pumpkin Bread

Under 200 Calories

Makes 1 loaf (16 slices)

1 cup quick-cooking oats, uncooked
1 cup hot low-fat milk
¾ cup canned pumpkin
2 eggs, beaten
¼ cup margarine, melted
2 cups all-purpose flour
1 cup sugar
1 tablespoon baking powder
1 teaspoon ground cinnamon
¼ teaspoon ground nutmeg
¼ teaspoon salt
1 cup raisins
½ cup chopped pecans

Preheat oven to 350°F. In large bowl, combine oats and milk; let stand about 5 minutes. Stir in pumpkin, eggs and melted margarine. In separate bowl, mix together flour, sugar, baking powder, cinnamon, nutmeg and salt. Gradually add dry ingredients to oatmeal mixture. Stir in raisins and nuts; mix well. Place in greased 9×5-inch loaf pan. Bake 55 to 60 minutes or until wooden toothpick inserted in center comes out clean. Cool on wire rack.

Nutrients per slice:

Calories	194	Sodium	135 mg
Fat	4 g	Cholesterol	35 mg

Favorite recipe from **The Sugar Association**.

Apple Sauce Bran Muffins

Low Cholesterol

Makes 1 dozen muffins

1½ cups NABISCO® 100% Bran™
1½ cups MOTT'S® Regular or Natural Apple
   Sauce
1 egg, slightly beaten
¼ cup margarine, melted
½ cup firmly packed light brown sugar
1½ cups all-purpose flour
1 tablespoon baking powder
1 teaspoon ground cinnamon
½ cup seedless raisins, optional
   Apple Sauce Glaze (recipe follows)

In large bowl, mix bran, apple sauce, egg, margarine and brown sugar; let stand 5 minutes. In separate bowl, blend flour, baking powder and cinnamon; stir in bran mixture just until blended (batter will be lumpy). Stir in raisins if desired. Spoon batter into 12 greased 2½-inch muffin-pan cups. Bake at 400°F for 15 to 18 minutes or until toothpick inserted in center comes out clean. Remove from pan. Cool slightly. Drizzle with Apple Sauce Glaze; serve warm.

Apple Sauce Glaze: Blend ½ cup confectioners' sugar into 1 tablespoon MOTT'S® Regular or Natural Apple Sauce until smooth.

Nutrients per muffin:

Calories	221	Sodium	232 mg
Fat	5 g	Cholesterol	18 mg

Blueberry Orange Loaf

Blueberry Orange Loaf

Under 200 Calories

Makes 12 slices

1 package DUNCAN HINES® Bakery Style
    Blueberry Muffin Mix
½ teaspoon baking powder
2 egg whites
⅔ cup CITRUS HILL® Orange Juice
1 teaspoon grated orange peel

1. Preheat oven to 350°F. Grease one 8×4-inch or 9×5-inch loaf pan.

2. Rinse blueberries from Mix with cold water and drain.

3. Empty muffin mix into bowl. Add baking powder; stir to combine and break up any lumps. Add egg whites and orange juice. Stir until moistened, about 50 strokes. Fold in blueberries and orange peel. Pour into pan. Sprinkle topping from Mix over batter. Bake at 350°F for 45 to 55 minutes or until toothpick inserted in center comes out clean. Cool in pan 10 minutes. Loosen loaf from pan. Invert onto cooling rack. Turn right side up. Cool completely.

Nutrients per slice:

Calories	189	Sodium	268 mg
Fat	5 g	Cholesterol	0 mg

Cranberry Oat Bran Muffins

Under 200 Calories

Makes 1 dozen muffins

2 cups flour
1 cup oat bran
½ cup packed brown sugar
2 teaspoons baking powder
½ teaspoon baking soda
½ teaspoon salt (optional)
½ cup MIRACLE WHIP® Cholesterol Free
    Dressing
3 egg whites, slightly beaten
½ cup skim milk
⅓ cup orange juice
1 teaspoon grated orange rind
1 cup coarsely chopped cranberries

Preheat oven to 375°. Line 12 medium muffin cups with paper baking cups or spray with vegetable cooking spray. Mix together dry ingredients. Add combined dressing, egg whites, milk, juice and rind, mixing just until moistened. Fold in cranberries. Fill prepared muffin cups almost full. Bake 15 to 17 minutes or until golden brown.

Nutrients per muffin:

Calories	190	Sodium	180 mg
Fat	5 g	Cholesterol	0 mg

Bavarian Rice Cloud with Bittersweet Chocolate Sauce

Cool
DELIGHTS

Bavarian Rice Cloud with Bittersweet Chocolate Sauce

Under 200 Calories

Makes 10 servings

1 envelope unflavored gelatin
1½ cups skim milk
3 tablespoons sugar
2 cups cooked rice
2 cups frozen light whipped topping, thawed
1 tablespoon almond-flavored liqueur
½ teaspoon vanilla extract
   Vegetable cooking spray
   Bittersweet Chocolate Sauce (recipe follows)
2 tablespoons sliced almonds, toasted

Sprinkle gelatin over milk in small saucepan; let stand 1 minute or until gelatin is softened. Cook over low heat, stirring constantly, until gelatin dissolves. Add sugar and stir until dissolved. Add rice; stir until well blended. Cover and chill until the consistency of unbeaten egg whites. Fold in whipped topping, liqueur, and vanilla. Spoon into 4-cup mold coated with cooking spray. Cover and chill until firm. To serve, unmold onto serving platter. Spoon chocolate sauce over rice dessert. Sprinkle with toasted almonds.

Bittersweet Chocolate Sauce

3 tablespoons unsweetened cocoa
3 tablespoons sugar
½ cup low-fat buttermilk
1 tablespoon almond-flavored liqueur

Combine cocoa and sugar in small saucepan. Add buttermilk, mixing well. Place over medium heat, and cook until sugar dissolves. Stir in liqueur; remove from heat.

Tip: Unmold gelatin desserts onto slightly dampened plate. This will allow you to move the mold and position it where you want it on the plate.

Nutrients per serving:

Calories	146	Sodium	211 mg
Fat	3 g	Cholesterol	1 mg

Favorite recipe from **USA Rice Council**.

Apricot Mousse

Low Cholesterol

Makes 6 servings

1 (32-ounce) container DANNON® Vanilla Lowfat Yogurt
2 cans (16 ounces *each*) apricot halves in heavy syrup
1 tablespoon sugar
1½ teaspoons orange-flavored liqueur (optional)
1 cup fresh blueberries, rinsed and drained
4 fresh strawberries, hulled and thinly sliced
   Mint sprigs for garnish (optional)

Line large strainer with double thickness of cheesecloth or triple layer of paper towels. Place strainer over large bowl to catch the liquid (whey) that will drain off. Spoon yogurt into strainer. Cover and refrigerate overnight. Scrape drained yogurt into medium bowl. Discard the whey. Drain apricots and process to a smooth purée in food processor or blender. Add to yogurt with sugar and liqueur; stir to mix well. Cover and chill at least 30 minutes. To serve, divide blueberries among 6 wine glasses or dessert dishes, reserving a few berries for the top. Spoon mousse over berries. Arrange a few strawberry slices over each glass. Sprinkle with remaining blueberries and garnish with mint.

Nutrients per serving:

Calories	200	Sodium	100 mg
Fat	3 g	Cholesterol	5 mg

Coconut Grove Mold

Under 200 Calories

Makes 8 servings

1 (8 oz.) can crushed pineapple in unsweetened
　juice, undrained
　Cold water
1 (3 oz.) pkg. JELL-O® Brand Pineapple Flavor
　Sugar Free Gelatin Dessert
1 (8 oz.) pkg. PHILADELPHIA BRAND®
　LIGHT Neufchatel Cheese, softened
⅓ cup BAKER'S® ANGEL FLAKE® Coconut

* Drain pineapple, reserving juice.

* Bring 1 cup water to boil. Gradually add to gelatin
in small bowl; stir until dissolved.

* Add enough water to reserved juice to measure
¾ cup. Stir into gelatin.

* Beat neufchatel cheese in large mixing bowl at
medium speed with electric mixer 1 minute.
Gradually add gelatin, mixing until well blended.
Chill until thickened but not set.

* Fold pineapple and coconut into neufchatel cheese
mixture; pour into lightly oiled 4-cup mold. Chill
until firm. Unmold.

Nutrients per serving:

Calories	110	Sodium	150 mg
Fat	8 g	Cholesterol	25 mg

Strawberry Ice

Under 200 Calories

Makes 6 servings

1 quart fresh strawberries, cleaned and hulled
　(about 1½ pounds)
1 cup sugar
½ cup water
3 tablespoons REALEMON® Lemon Juice from
　Concentrate
　Red food coloring, optional

In blender container, combine sugar, water and
ReaLemon® brand; mix well. Gradually add
strawberries; blend until smooth, adding food coloring
if desired. Pour into 8-inch square pan; freeze about
1½ hours. In small mixer bowl, beat until slushy.
Return to freezer in square pan. Place in refrigerator
1 hour before serving to soften. Freeze leftovers.

Nutrients per serving:

Calories	162	Sodium	3 mg
Fat	0 g	Cholesterol	0 mg

Zinfandel Sorbet with Poached Pears

Under 200 Calories

Makes 8 servings

Zinfandel Sorbet
　1 envelope KNOX® Unflavored Gelatine
　½ cup cold water
　⅓ cup sugar
1¼ cups white Zinfandel wine
　1 can (5½ ounces) pear nectar

Poached Pears
　2 cups white Zinfandel wine
　¾ cup sugar
　1 tablespoon lemon juice
　4 medium Anjou or Bartlett pears, peeled, halved
　　and cored

Zinfandel Sorbet: In medium saucepan, sprinkle
unflavored gelatine over cold water; let stand 1
minute. Stir over low heat until gelatine is completely
dissolved, about 3 minutes. Stir in sugar until
dissolved, then stir in remaining ingredients. Pour into
9-inch square baking pan; freeze 3 hours or until
firm. With electric mixer or food processor, beat
mixture until smooth. Return to pan; freeze 6 hours
or until firm. Serve sorbet in Poached Pears drizzled
with Poached Pears syrup, or serve in stemmed
glassware. Garnish, if desired, with fresh mint.

Poached Pears: In large skillet, thoroughly blend
wine, sugar and lemon juice. Add pear halves, cut-side
down, and simmer covered 15 minutes or until pears
are tender. Remove pears and chill. Cook remaining
liquid, uncovered, over medium-high heat 10 minutes
or until liquid is reduced by half; chill.

Nutrients per serving with Poached Pears:

Calories	197	Sodium	7 mg
Fat	0 g	Cholesterol	0 mg

Nutrients per serving for Zinfandel Sorbet only:

Calories	73	Sodium	4 mg
Fat	0 g	Cholesterol	0 mg

Zinfandel Sorbet with Poached Pears

From left to right: Cranberry Apple Ice, Orange Apple Ice and Apple Honeydew Ice

Cranberry Apple Ice

Under 100 Calories

Makes 14 (½-cup) servings

1 (12-ounce) can frozen apple-cranberry juice
  concentrate, thawed
1½ cups MOTT'S® Chunky Apple Sauce
1 (32-ounce) bottle (4 cups) sugar-free lemon-
  lime flavored carbonated beverage

In 2-quart non-metal bowl, combine all ingredients;
mix well. Cover; freeze until firm. Scoop frozen
mixture into 5-ounce drink cups or spoon into dessert
dishes.

Nutrients per serving:			
Calories	33	Sodium	14 mg
Fat	0 g	Cholesterol	0 mg

Orange Apple Ice

Under 100 Calories

Makes 12 (½-cup) servings

1 (23-ounce) jar MOTT'S® Natural or Regular
  Apple Sauce
⅓ cup orange marmalade
3 egg whites, beaten stiff°

In medium bowl, combine apple sauce and
marmalade; mix well. Carefully fold in beaten egg
whites. Pour into 8- or 9-inch square pan. Cover;
freeze until firm. Scoop frozen mixture into 5-ounce
cups, dessert dishes or orange shells (see Tip).

Tip: To make shell or cup, use a sharp knife to make
sawtooth-cut around middle of fruit, cutting inside to
center only. Twist, pull apart and remove inside
portion, scraping shells clean with spoon.

°*Use only clean, uncracked eggs.*

Nutrients per serving:			
Calories	51	Sodium	15 mg
Fat	0 g	Cholesterol	0 mg

Apple Honeydew Ice

Under 100 Calories

Makes 10 (½-cup) servings

- 2 cups sugar-free lemon-lime flavored carbonated beverage
- 1 cup MOTT'S® Regular Apple Sauce
- 1 small honeydew melon, seeded, rind removed, cut into chunks
- ⅛ teaspoon ground ginger
- 2 to 3 drops green food color, if desired

In food processor or blender, combine all ingredients; process until smooth. Pour into 8- or 9-inch non-metal square pan. Cover; freeze until firm. Scoop frozen mixture into 5-ounce cups or into dessert dishes.

Nutrients per serving:			
Calories	37	Sodium	14 mg
Fat	0 g	Cholesterol	0 mg

Peanutty Pudding Pops

Low Cholesterol

Makes 6 pops

- 1 envelope KNOX® Unflavored Gelatine
- 1 cup cold skim milk
- 1 cup boiling water
- ½ cup sugar
- ⅓ cup peanut butter
- ⅛ teaspoon ground cinnamon
  Suggested Pudding Toppers

In blender, sprinkle unflavored gelatine over cold milk; let stand 2 minutes. Add boiling water and process at low speed until gelatine is completely dissolved, about 2 minutes. Add sugar, peanut butter and cinnamon; process at high speed until blended, about 15 seconds. Spoon 1 tablespoon Suggested Pudding Toppers into each of 6 (5-ounce) paper cups; pour in pudding mixture. Freeze until partially frozen, about 1 hour. Insert wooden ice cream sticks; freeze until firm, about 4 hours. To serve, let stand at room temperature 2 minutes; tear away cup.

Suggested Pudding Toppers: Use any of the following: chocolate chips, crushed cookies or granola, raisins or peanuts.

Nutrients per pop:			
Calories	211	Sodium	89 mg
Fat	10 g	Cholesterol	1 mg

Frozen Banana Dessert Cups

Low Sodium

Makes 8 to 12 servings

- 2 extra-ripe, medium DOLE® Bananas
- 1 cup DOLE® fresh or frozen Strawberries
- 1 can (8 ounces) DOLE® Crushed Pineapple in juice, drained
- 2 tablespoons honey
  Dash ground nutmeg
- 1 cup frozen whipped topping, thawed
- ¼ cup DOLE® Chopped Almonds
- 1 cup DOLE® Pure & Light Mountain Cherry Juice
- 1 tablespoon cornstarch
- 1 tablespoon sugar
  Sliced DOLE® fresh fruit, for garnish

- Place bananas, strawberries, pineapple, honey and nutmeg in blender. Process until smooth. Fold in whipped topping and almonds.

- Line 12 muffin cups with foil liners. Fill with banana mixture. Cover and freeze until firm.

- Blend cherry juice, cornstarch and sugar in small saucepan. Cook, stirring, until sauce boils and thickens. Cool.

- To serve, spoon cherry sauce onto each serving plate. Remove foil liners from dessert. Invert on top of sauce. Arrange fresh fruit around mold.

Nutrients per serving:			
Calories	99	Sodium	4 mg
Fat	3 g	Cholesterol	0 mg

Frozen Banana Dessert Cup

Chilled Lemonade Dessert

Makes 8 servings

1½ cups cold water
1 (3 oz.) pkg. JELL-O® Brand Lemon Flavor
   Sugar Free Gelatin Dessert
1 (8 oz.) pkg. PHILADELPHIA BRAND®
   LIGHT Neufchatel Cheese, softened
⅓ cup frozen lemonade concentrate, thawed
1 teaspoon grated lemon peel
2 cups COOL WHIP® Non-Dairy Whipped
   Topping, thawed

- Bring water to boil. Gradually add to gelatin in small bowl; stir until dissolved.

- Beat neufchatel cheese, lemonade concentrate and peel in large mixing bowl at medium speed with electric mixer until well blended. Stir in gelatin; chill until thickened but not set.

- Fold in whipped topping; pour into lightly oiled 6-cup mold. Chill until firm. Unmold. Garnish with peach slices, blueberries and fresh mint leaves, if desired.

Variation: Substitute eight individual ½-cup molds for 6-cup mold.

Nutrients per serving:			
Calories	160	Sodium	150 mg
Fat	10 g	Cholesterol	25 mg

Chilled Lemonade Dessert

Peach Ice Cream

Makes 7 cups

7 fresh California peaches
1 envelope unflavored gelatin
2 cups low-fat milk
1 cup plain low-fat yogurt
½ cup sugar
1 tablespoon vanilla extract

Chop enough peaches to measure 1 cup. Purée remaining peaches in blender or food processor to measure 2½ cups. Sprinkle gelatin over milk in medium saucepan. Let stand 1 minute to soften. Stir over medium heat until gelatin dissolves; remove from heat. Add chopped peaches, peach purée, yogurt, sugar and vanilla extract to gelatin mixture; mix well. Prepare in ice cream maker according to manufacturer's instructions. Pack into containers. Freeze until firm.

Nutrients per ½ cup serving:			
Calories	85	Sodium	30 mg
Fat	1 g	Cholesterol	4 mg

Favorite recipe from **California Tree Fruit Agreement**.

Banana Kiwi Pudding

Makes 4 servings

1⅓ cups cooked rice
1⅓ cups skim milk
1 teaspoon vanilla extract
   Low-calorie sugar substitute to equal
    2 tablespoons sugar
1 ripe banana
¼ cup whipping cream, whipped
2 kiwifruits, sliced, for garnish

Cook rice and milk in 2-quart saucepan over medium heat until thick and creamy, 5 to 8 minutes, stirring frequently. Remove from heat; cool. Stir in vanilla and sugar substitute. Just before serving, mash banana; fold banana and whipped cream into pudding. Garnish with kiwifruit slices.

Nutrients per serving:			
Calories	197	Sodium	306 mg
Fat	4 g	Cholesterol	12 mg

Favorite recipe from **USA Rice Council**.

Jell-O® Sugar Free Jigglers

Jell-O® Sugar Free Jigglers

Under 100 Calories

Makes 8 dozen cubes

2½ cups boiling water
    4 packages (4-serving size each) or 2 packages
    (8-serving size each) JELL-O® Brand Sugar
    Free Gelatin, any flavor

ADD boiling water to gelatin. Dissolve completely.
Pour into 13×9-inch pan. Chill until firm, about 3
hours.

DIP pan in warm water about 15 seconds for easy
removal. Cut gelatin into 1-inch squares. (Or use
cookie cutters to cut decorative shapes; cut remaining
gelatin into cubes.)

Notes: For thicker Jell-O® Sugar Free Jigglers, use
8- or 9-inch square pan.

To use ice cube trays or Jell-O® Jiggler molds, pour
gelatin mixture into 2 or 3 ice cube trays. Chill until
firm, about 2 hours. To remove, dip trays in warm
water about 15 seconds. Moisten tips of fingers and
gently pull from edges.

Nutrients per cube:			
Calories	2	Sodium	10 mg
Fat	0 g	Cholesterol	0 mg

Melon Bubbles

Melon Bubbles

Under 100 Calories

Makes 7 (½-cup) servings

1 package (4-serving size) JELL-O® Brand Sugar
    Free Gelatin, any flavor
¾ cup boiling water
½ cup cold water
    Ice cubes
1 cup melon balls (cantaloupe, honeydew or
    watermelon)
    Mint leaves (optional)

DISSOLVE gelatin in boiling water. Combine cold
water and ice cubes to make 1¼ cups. Add to gelatin,
stirring until slightly thickened. Remove any unmelted
ice. Measure 1⅓ cups gelatin into small bowl; add
melon. Pour into dessert dishes or serving bowl.

WHIP remaining gelatin at high speed of electric
mixer until fluffy, thick and about doubled in volume.
Spoon over gelatin in glasses. Chill until set, about 2
hours. Garnish with additional melon balls and mint
leaves, if desired.

Nutrients per serving:

Calories	14	Sodium	50 mg
Fat	0 g	Cholesterol	0 mg

Lemon Rice Dessert

Under 200 Calories

Makes 8 servings

1 package (3 ounces) lemon-flavored gelatin
    dessert
1 cup boiling water
½ cup cold water
1 cup cooked rice, chilled
1½ cups frozen whipped topping, thawed
¼ cup sliced almonds
¼ cup chopped maraschino cherries
1 tablespoon grated lemon peel

Dissolve gelatin in boiling water; add cold water.
Place bowl in ice water and stir until gelatin is the
consistency of unbeaten egg whites; stir in rice. Fold
in whipped topping until smooth. Lightly fold in
almonds, cherries, and lemon peel. Continue to stir
gently (over ice) until thickened. Pour into dessert
dishes. Cover and chill until ready to serve.

Nutrients per serving:

Calories	131	Sodium	149 mg
Fat	3 g	Cholesterol	2 mg

Favorite recipe from **USA Rice Council**.

Chocolate Raspberry Sorbet

Under 100 Calories

Makes 1½ pints

2 cups water, divided
½ cup sugar
⅓ cup NESTLÉ® Cocoa
1½ cups fresh or thawed frozen raspberries

In small saucepan, combine 1 cup of the water and
the sugar. Bring to a boil, stirring constantly, until
sugar dissolves. Boil 2 minutes, without stirring. With
wire whisk, stir in cocoa until smooth. Add remaining
1 cup water; cool.

In blender or food processor, purée cocoa mixture
with raspberries until smooth. Press purée through
fine sieve to remove seeds. Pour into 9-inch square
metal baking pan; freeze until a firm slush forms.
Spoon slush into chilled bowl of food processor or
electric mixer; process or beat until ice crystals
become very fine. Return to freezer until firm. Let
stand at room temperature about 10 minutes before
serving.

Nutrients per ½ cup serving:

Calories	95	Sodium	3 mg
Fat	1 g	Cholesterol	0 mg

Pumpkin Pie Ice Cream

Under 200 Calories

Makes 1½ quarts

3 cups (two 12-ounce cans) *undiluted*
    CARNATION® Evaporated Milk
1¾ cups (16-ounce can) LIBBY'S® Solid Pack
    Pumpkin
1½ cups granulated sugar
½ teaspoon pumpkin pie spice
⅛ teaspoon salt

In blender container, place evaporated milk, pumpkin,
sugar, pumpkin pie spice, and salt; blend on low
speed. Pour into ice cream maker and freeze
according to manufacturer's instructions.

Variation: For fruit or berry ice cream, combine in
large bowl, 2 cups fruit pulp,° 3 cups evaporated milk,
1½ cups sugar, 2 teaspoons lemon juice, and ⅛
teaspoon salt. Freeze as above. *Makes about 2 quarts.*

°*Any fruit or berries may be used. If using sweetened
frozen fruit, reduce sugar to ½ cup.*

Nutrients per ½ cup serving:

Calories	195	Sodium	90 mg
Fat	5 g	Cholesterol	19 mg

Rice Pudding

Makes 6 servings

3 cups 2% low-fat milk
1 large stick cinnamon
1 cup uncooked long-grain white rice
2 cups water
½ teaspoon salt
  Peel of an orange or lemon
¾ cup sugar
¼ cup raisins
2 tablespoons dark rum

Heat milk and cinnamon in small saucepan over medium heat until milk is infused with flavor of cinnamon, about 15 minutes. Combine rice, water, and salt in 2- to 3-quart saucepan. Bring to a boil; stir once or twice. Place orange peel on top of rice. Reduce heat, cover, and simmer 15 minutes or until rice is tender and liquid is absorbed. Remove and discard orange peel. Strain milk and stir into cooked rice. Add sugar and simmer 20 minutes or until thickened, stirring often. Add raisins and rum; simmer 10 minutes. Serve cold or hot. To reheat, add a little milk to restore creamy texture.

Tip: Use medium or short grain rice for rice pudding with a creamier consistency.

Nutrients per serving:			
Calories	297	Sodium	259 mg
Fat	3 g	Cholesterol	10 mg

Favorite recipe from **USA Rice Council.**

Strawberry Pops

Makes 8 pops

1 envelope KNOX® Unflavored Gelatine
¾ cup cold skim milk
1 cup boiling water
2 cups frozen strawberries
½ cup sugar

In blender, sprinkle unflavored gelatine over cold milk; let stand 2 minutes. Add boiling water and process at low speed until gelatine is completely dissolved, about 2 minutes. Add strawberries and sugar; process at high speed until smooth. Pour into 8 (5-ounce) paper cups; freeze until partially frozen, about 1 hour. Insert wooden ice cream sticks; freeze until firm, about 4 hours. To serve, let stand at room temperature 2 minutes; tear away cup.

Nutrients per pop:			
Calories	73	Sodium	14 mg
Fat	0 g	Cholesterol	0 mg

Raspberry Rice aux Amandes

Makes 8 servings

3 cups cooked rice
2 cups skim milk
⅛ teaspoon salt
  Low-calorie sugar substitute to equal
    2 tablespoons sugar
1 teaspoon vanilla extract
¾ cup frozen light whipped topping, thawed
3 tablespoons sliced almonds, toasted
1 package (16 ounces) frozen unsweetened
    raspberries, thawed°

Combine rice, milk, and salt in 2-quart saucepan. Cook over medium heat until thick and creamy, 5 to 8 minutes, stirring frequently. Remove from heat. Cool. Add sugar substitute and vanilla. Fold in whipped topping and almonds. Alternate rice mixture and raspberries in parfait glasses or dessert dishes.

To microwave: Combine rice, milk, and salt in 1½-quart microproof baking dish. Cover and cook on HIGH 3 minutes. Reduce setting to MEDIUM (50% power) and cook 7 minutes, stirring after 3 and 5 minutes. Stir in sugar substitute and vanilla; cool. Fold in whipped topping and almonds. Alternate rice mixture and raspberries in parfait glasses or dessert dishes.

°*Substitute frozen unsweetened strawberries or other fruit for the raspberries, if desired.*

Nutrients per serving:			
Calories	180	Sodium	369 mg
Fat	3 g	Cholesterol	2 mg

Favorite recipe from **USA Rice Council.**

Fresh Peach Sorbet

Makes about 1 quart

7 fresh California peaches, quartered
¾ cup sugar
3 tablespoons light corn syrup
1 teaspoon lemon juice

Purée peaches in blender or food processor to measure 3½ cups. Combine peach purée, sugar, corn syrup and lemon juice in saucepan. Cook over low heat until sugar dissolves. Cool to room temperature. Prepare in ice cream maker according to manufacturer's instructions. Pack into containers. Freeze until firm.

Nutrients per ¼ cup serving:			
Calories	69	Sodium	3 mg
Fat	0 g	Cholesterol	0 mg

Favorite recipe from **California Tree Fruit Agreement.**

Rice Pudding

Lite Chocolate Mint Parfaits

Makes 7 servings

⅔ cup sugar
¼ cup HERSHEY'S® Cocoa
3 tablespoons cornstarch
   Dash salt
2½ cups cold skim milk, divided
1 tablespoon margarine
1½ teaspoons vanilla extract, divided
1 envelope whipped topping mix (to make 2 cups whipped topping)
¼ teaspoon mint extract
3 to 4 drops green food color (optional)

In medium saucepan, combine sugar, cocoa, cornstarch and salt; gradually stir in 2 cups of the milk. Cook over medium heat, stirring constantly, until mixture boils; boil and stir 1 minute. Remove from heat; blend in margarine and 1 teaspoon of the vanilla. Pour into medium bowl. Press plastic wrap directly onto surface of pudding; refrigerate. In small bowl, combine topping mix, remaining ½ cup milk and ½ teaspoon vanilla; prepare according to package directions. Fold ½ cup of the topping into pudding. Blend mint extract and green food color into remaining topping. Alternately spoon chocolate pudding and mint whipped topping into parfait glasses. Refrigerate until thoroughly chilled.

Nutrients per serving:			
Calories	175	Sodium	104 mg
Fat	4 g	Cholesterol	2 mg

Cranberry Sorbet

Makes 6 servings

1 package OCEAN SPRAY® Cran-Fruit™ Sauce
2 cups OCEAN SPRAY® Cranberry Juice Cocktail
1 cup corn syrup

In large bowl, combine all ingredients. Pour into 13×9-inch pan and freeze until firm. Cut mixture into small pieces. Process in food processor until smooth and light. Pour back into pan and refreeze until firm.

Nutrients per serving:			
Calories	300	Sodium	36 mg
Fat	0 g	Cholesterol	0 mg

Creamy Frozen Yogurt

Makes 7 (½-cup) servings

1 package (4-serving size) JELL-O® Brand Sugar Free Gelatin, any flavor
1 cup boiling water
½ cup cold water
1 container (8 ounces) plain lowfat yogurt
2 cups thawed COOL WHIP® Whipped Topping

DISSOLVE gelatin in boiling water. Add cold water. Stir in yogurt until well blended and smooth. Fold in whipped topping. Pour into 9-inch square pan. Freeze until firm, about 6 hours or overnight. Scoop into individual dessert dishes.

Nutrients per serving:			
Calories	80	Sodium	60 mg
Fat	4 g	Cholesterol	5 mg

Sweet Cream Puddings

Makes 6 (½-cup) servings

1 envelope KNOX® Unflavored Gelatine
¼ cup cold skim milk
½ cup skim milk, heated to boiling
1 cup (8 ounces) lite ricotta cheese
1 cup (8 ounces) 1% milkfat cottage cheese
½ cup sugar
1 teaspoon vanilla extract
½ cup frozen strawberries, thawed
¼ cup mini semi-sweet chocolate chips

In blender, sprinkle unflavored gelatine over cold milk; let stand 2 minutes. Add hot milk and process at low speed until gelatine is completely dissolved, about 2 minutes. Add ricotta, cottage cheese, sugar and vanilla; process at high speed until thoroughly blended, about 2 minutes. Equally pour into 2 medium bowls; set aside.

In same blender, purée strawberries; strain, if desired. Thoroughly combine strawberry purée with cheese mixture in one bowl. Chill plain and strawberry cheese mixtures until both are set, about 3 hours. To serve, whisk each mixture until smooth. Stir chocolate chips into plain mixture. Spoon mixtures side-by-side into each of 6 dessert cups.

Nutrients per serving:			
Calories	197	Sodium	218 mg
Fat	5 g	Cholesterol	9 mg

Satin Chocolate Mousse

Satin Chocolate Mousse

Under 200 Calories

Makes 4 servings

1 teaspoon KNOX® Unflavored Gelatine
¼ cup cold skim milk
½ cup skim milk, heated to boiling
¼ cup semi-sweet chocolate chips
1 container (8 ounces) 1% milkfat cottage cheese
¼ cup sugar
1 teaspoon vanilla extract

In blender, sprinkle unflavored gelatine over cold milk; let stand 2 minutes. Add hot milk and process at low speed until gelatine is completely dissolved, about 2 minutes. Add chocolate and process at high speed until completely melted, about 1 minute. Add remaining ingredients and process at high speed until blended. Pour into medium serving bowl or individual cups; chill until set, about 2 hours.

Variation: After chilled, whisk until smooth and serve as a dip or pour over fresh fruit, cubed angel food or pound cake.

Nutrients per serving:

Calories	167	Sodium	255 mg
Fat	4 g	Cholesterol	3 mg

Grape Yogurt Pops

Under 200 Calories

Makes 8 servings

2 cups (1 pint) plain lowfat yogurt
1 can (6 ounces) frozen orange juice concentrate, thawed
⅓ cup sugar
2 cups California seedless grapes

Combine yogurt, orange juice concentrate and sugar in large bowl; stir until concentrate is smooth and sugar dissolves. Pour into 8 (4-ounce) waxed paper cups. Drop ¼ cup grapes into each cup. Freeze until almost firm. Insert wooden ice cream stick in center of each cup. Freeze until firm. To serve, peel off cup.

Note: For longer storage, wrap pops in plastic wrap to prevent dehydration.

Nutrients per serving:

Calories	146	Sodium	42 mg
Fat	1 g	Cholesterol	3 mg

Favorite recipe from **California Table Grape Commission**.

Frozen Apple Sauce 'n Fruit Cup

Frozen Apple Sauce 'n Fruit Cup

Makes 7 (½-cup) servings

1 cup MOTT'S® Chunky or Regular Apple Sauce
1 (10-ounce) package frozen strawberries, thawed
1 (11-ounce) can mandarin orange segments, drained
1 cup grapes
2 tablespoons orange juice concentrate

In medium bowl, combine all ingredients. Spoon fruit mixture into individual dishes or paper cups. Freeze until firm. Remove from freezer about 30 minutes before serving.

Nutrients per serving:			
Calories	107	Sodium	5 mg
Fat	0 g	Cholesterol	0 mg

Sparkling Lemon-Lime Sorbet

Makes 6 servings

1 envelope KNOX® Unflavored Gelatine
½ cup sugar
1 cup water
1 cup Champagne, sauternes or ginger ale
½ cup fresh lemon juice (about 3 lemons)
⅓ cup fresh lime juice (about 3 limes)

In medium saucepan, mix unflavored gelatine with sugar; blend in water. Let stand 1 minute. Stir over low heat until gelatine is completely dissolved, about 5 minutes. Let cool to room temperature; stir in remaining ingredients. Pour into 9-inch square pan; freeze 3 hours or until firm.

With electric mixer or food processor, beat mixture until smooth. Return to pan; freeze 2 hours or until firm. To serve, let stand at room temperature 15 minutes or until slightly softened. Spoon into dessert dishes or stemmed glassware. Garnish, if desired, with fresh mint.

Nutrients per serving:			
Calories	99	Sodium	3 mg
Fat	0 g	Cholesterol	0 mg

Lemon Banana Yogurt Pops

Makes 6 servings

2 egg whites°
2 tablespoons sugar
1 ripe banana
2 cartons (8 ounces each) low-fat lemon-flavored yogurt

In small bowl, beat egg whites until soft peaks form. Gradually add sugar, beating until stiff peaks form. In blender or food processor, combine banana and yogurt; process until smooth. In large bowl, fold egg white mixture into yogurt mixture. Divide mixture among 6 ice cream molds or 5-ounce paper cups. Insert wooden ice cream sticks. Freeze until solid. Remove from molds or peel away paper cups.

°*Use only clean, uncracked eggs.*

Nutrients per serving:			
Calories	120	Sodium	61 mg
Fat	1 g	Cholesterol	3 mg

Favorite recipe from **The Sugar Association**.

Ambrosia Fruit Custard

Makes 4 servings

1 package (4-serving size) sugar-free instant vanilla pudding
  Ingredients for pudding
1 teaspoon DOLE® Lemon zest
1 tablespoon DOLE® Lemon juice
½ teaspoon coconut or almond extract
1 can (8 ounces) DOLE® Pineapple Tidbits in juice, drained
1 cup assorted sliced DOLE® fresh fruit
¼ cup mini marshmallows or flaked coconut

• Make pudding according to package directions in bowl. Stir in lemon zest, lemon juice and coconut extract. Reserve ¼ cup pudding for topping.

• Spoon remaining pudding equally into dessert bowls. Combine remaining ingredients in bowl. Spoon on top of pudding. Top with reserved pudding.

Nutrients per serving:			
Calories	139	Sodium	203 mg
Fat	2 g	Cholesterol	0 mg

Nectarine Raspberry Ice

Nectarine Raspberry Ice

Under 100 Calories

Makes about 2 quarts

1 envelope unflavored gelatin
½ cup cold water
½ cup dry white wine
⅓ cup sugar
1 package (10 ounces) unsweetened frozen
  raspberries, thawed
4 fresh California nectarines, cut into chunks
1 teaspoon lemon zest
¼ cup lemon juice

Sprinkle gelatin over water in saucepan. Let stand 1 minute to soften. Stir over medium heat until gelatin dissolves. Stir in wine and sugar; cook and stir until sugar is dissolved. Remove from heat; set aside. Purée raspberries, nectarines, lemon zest and lemon juice in blender. Combine with wine syrup. Turn into shallow pan and freeze until firm. Soften slightly, then beat smooth with mixer. Refreeze and keep frozen until ready to serve.

Nutrients per ½ cup serving:

Calories	62	Sodium	1 mg
Fat	0 g	Cholesterol	0 mg

Favorite recipe from **California Tree Fruit Agreement.**

Lime Sorbet

Under 100 Calories

Makes 6 servings

4 large limes
1½ cups hot water
6 tablespoons sugar
1 egg white, slightly beaten°
1 drop *each* green and yellow food color
  Mint leaves or citrus leaves, for garnish

Grate the peel from 1 lime; reserve. Squeeze juice from limes to measure ½ cup juice. In 1-quart measure, combine hot water and sugar; stir to dissolve. In medium bowl, combine lime juice, lime peel, sugar mixture, egg white and food color; blend well. Pour into shallow pan. Cover and freeze, stirring about once an hour to break up ice crystals, until firm. Remove sorbet from freezer about 10 minutes before serving.

°*Use only clean, uncracked egg.*

Nutrients per serving:

Calories	68	Sodium	9 mg
Fat	1 g	Cholesterol	0 mg

Favorite recipe from **The Sugar Association.**

Alpine Strawberry Bavarian

Under 200 Calories

Makes 12 servings

1½ cups water
2 (3 oz.) pkgs. JELL-O® Brand Lemon Flavor
  Sugar Free Gelatin Dessert
1½ cups cold water
1 (8 oz.) container PHILADELPHIA BRAND®
  LIGHT Pasteurized Process Cream Cheese
  Product
1 pt. strawberry ice milk or ice cream, softened
1 tablespoon lemon juice
2 cups strawberry slices

• Bring 1½ cups water to boil. Gradually add gelatin in medium bowl; stir until dissolved. Stir in 1½ cups cold water.

• Gradually add gelatin to cream cheese product in large mixing bowl, mixing at medium speed with electric mixer until well blended.

• Stir in ice milk and lemon juice; fold in strawberries. Spoon into twelve parfait glasses or 1½-quart bowl. Chill.

• Garnish each serving with whipped topping, chocolate curls and strawberries, if desired.

Nutrients per serving:

Calories	100	Sodium	130 mg
Fat	5 g	Cholesterol	10 mg

Cocoa Chiffon Dessert

Under 100 Calories

Makes 8 servings

1 envelope unflavored gelatin
3 tablespoons sugar
3 tablespoons **HERSHEY'S®** Cocoa
1¾ cups skim milk
½ teaspoon vanilla extract
1 envelope dry whipped topping mix (to make 2 cups whipped topping)
½ cup cold skim milk

In medium saucepan, mix gelatin with sugar; add cocoa. Blend in 1¾ cups milk; let stand 5 minutes. Stir over low heat with wire whisk until gelatin is completely dissolved, about 5 minutes. Remove from heat; stir in vanilla. Refrigerate until mixture begins to thicken. In medium bowl, combine topping mix and ½ cup cold milk; prepare according to package directions. Fold 1½ cups whipped topping into cocoa mixture. Spoon into dessert dishes. Cover; refrigerate until firm. Garnish with remaining topping.

Variation: 1 teaspoon brandy extract may be substituted for vanilla.

Nutrients per serving:			
Calories	78	Sodium	35 mg
Fat	2 g	Cholesterol	1 mg

Orange Lemon Sorbet

Under 200 Calories

Makes 6 servings

1 cup sugar
1 cup water
1½ cups orange juice
⅓ cup **REALEMON®** Lemon Juice from Concentrate
1 teaspoon grated orange rind
2 tablespoons orange-flavored liqueur, optional

In medium saucepan, combine sugar and water. Over medium heat, bring to a boil; boil 5 minutes. Remove from heat; chill 20 minutes. Add remaining ingredients to sugar syrup. Pour into 8- or 9-inch square pan; freeze about 1½ hours or until slightly frozen. In large mixer bowl, beat until smooth; return to pan. Cover. Freeze at least 1½ hours before serving. If storing longer, remove from freezer 5 minutes before serving. Return leftovers to freezer.

Nutrients per serving:			
Calories	159	Sodium	4 mg
Fat	0 g	Cholesterol	0 mg

Peach Melba Parfaits

Low Cholesterol

Makes 6 parfaits

1 (10-ounce) package frozen red raspberries in syrup, thawed
¼ cup red currant jelly
1 tablespoon cornstarch
½ (½-gallon carton) **BORDEN®** or **MEADOW GOLD®** Peach Frozen Yogurt
⅔ cup granola or natural cereal

Drain raspberries, reserving ⅔ cup syrup. In small saucepan, combine reserved syrup, jelly and cornstarch. Cook and stir until slightly thickened and glossy. Cool. Stir in raspberries. In parfait or wine glasses, layer raspberry sauce, frozen yogurt, raspberry sauce then granola; repeat. Freeze. Remove from freezer 5 to 10 minutes before serving. Garnish as desired. Freeze leftovers.

Nutrients per serving:			
Calories	268	Sodium	75 mg
Fat	5 g	Cholesterol	9 mg

Peach Melba Parfaits

Strawberries Elegante and Spectacular Cannolis (page 33)

Fruitful ◆◆◆ PLEASURES

Strawberries Elegante

Under 200 Calories

Makes 6 servings

    6 cups strawberry slices
    2 tablespoons orange flavored liqueur or orange
        juice
    1 (8 oz.) container PHILADELPHIA BRAND®
        LIGHT Pasteurized Process Cream Cheese
        Product
    3 tablespoons brown sugar
    1 tablespoon orange flavored liqueur or orange
        juice
    1 tablespoon skim milk

- Toss strawberries with 2 tablespoons liqueur in small
bowl.

- Place cream cheese product, sugar, 1 tablespoon
liqueur and milk in food processor or blender
container; process until well blended. Serve over
strawberries. Garnish with fresh mint leaves, if
desired.

Nutrients per serving:			
Calories	170	Sodium	220 mg
Fat	7 g	Cholesterol	20 mg

Apricot Crumble

Under 200 Calories

Makes 12 servings

    1 cup dried apricots
    1¼ cups water
    2 tablespoons brown sugar (optional)
    1½ cups all-purpose flour
    ½ cup firmly packed brown sugar
    ¼ teaspoon salt (optional)
    ¼ teaspoon cinnamon
    ⅓ cup margarine
    1 cup KELLOGG'S® ALL-BRAN® cereal
    3 tablespoons water

1. In 2-quart saucepan, simmer apricots in 1¼ cups
water, uncovered, about 20 minutes or until tender.
Purée apricots, cooking liquid and 2 tablespoons
brown sugar in blender or food processor; set aside.

2. While apricots are simmering, in large mixing bowl,
combine flour, ½ cup brown sugar, salt and cinnamon.
Using pastry blender, cut in margarine until mixture
resembles coarse crumbs. Stir in Kellogg's® All-Bran®
cereal; mix well. Add the 3 tablespoons water
(mixture will be crumbly). Set aside 1 cup cereal
mixture. With back of spoon, press remaining cereal
mixture firmly into bottom of ungreased 9-inch square
baking pan. Spread puréed apricots evenly over cereal
mixture in pan. Sprinkle with reserved cereal mixture,
pressing slightly.

3. Bake in 350°F oven about 35 minutes or until
lightly browned. Cool completely. Cut into squares to
serve.

Nutrients per serving:			
Calories	190	Sodium	188 mg
Fat	5 g	Cholesterol	0 mg

Blueberry Crisp

Blueberry Crisp

Low Cholesterol

Makes 8 servings

3 cups cooked brown rice
3 cups fresh blueberries°
¼ cup + 3 tablespoons firmly packed brown
    sugar, divided
    Vegetable cooking spray
⅓ cup rice bran
¼ cup whole-wheat flour
¼ cup chopped walnuts
1 teaspoon ground cinnamon
3 tablespoons margarine

Combine rice, blueberries, and 3 tablespoons brown sugar. Coat 8 individual custard cups or 2-quart baking dish with cooking spray. Place rice mixture in cups or baking dish; set aside. Combine bran, flour, walnuts, remaining ¼ cup sugar, and cinnamon in bowl. Cut in margarine with pastry blender until mixture resembles coarse meal. Sprinkle over rice mixture. Bake at 375°F. for 15 to 20 minutes or until thoroughly heated. Serve warm.

To microwave: Prepare as directed using 2-quart microproof baking dish. Cook, uncovered, on HIGH 4 to 5 minutes, rotating dish once during cooking time. Let stand 5 minutes. Serve warm.

°*Substitute frozen unsweetened blueberries for the fresh blueberries, if desired. Thaw and drain before using. Or, substitute your choice of fresh fruit or combinations of fruit for the blueberries, if desired.*

Nutrients per serving:

Calories	243	Sodium	61 mg
Fat	8 g	Cholesterol	0 mg

Favorite recipe from **USA Rice Council.**

Crispy Baked Apple Slices

Low Sodium

Makes 6 servings

2½ pounds (5 to 6 large) Golden Delicious or
    Rome Beauty apples, peeled and sliced
    (about 5 cups)
2 tablespoons apple juice
½ cup all-purpose flour
½ cup firmly packed light brown sugar
½ teaspoon cinnamon
¼ cup **BUTTER FLAVOR CRISCO®**

1. Preheat oven to 375°F. Grease 2-quart ovenproof
dish.

2. Arrange apples evenly in dish. Pour apple juice
over apples.

3. Combine flour, brown sugar and cinnamon in small
bowl. Mix in Butter Flavor Crisco® until crumbly.
Spoon evenly over apples. Bake at 375°F for 35
minutes or until apples are tender. Cool slightly. Serve
warm either plain or topped with a spoonful of vanilla
yogurt, if desired.

Nutrients per serving:			
Calories	289	Sodium	10 mg
Fat	9 g	Cholesterol	0 mg

Microwave Streusel Pears

Low Cholesterol

Makes 6 servings

6 cups sliced, firm fresh pears (about 6 medium)
3 tablespoons granulated sugar
1 tablespoon fresh lemon juice
1 cup quick-cooking oats
⅓ cup firmly packed brown sugar
2 tablespoons flour
½ teaspoon ground cinnamon
¼ teaspoon ground nutmeg
¼ cup margarine

In large bowl, toss pears with granulated sugar and
lemon juice. Spray 8-inch square microwave-safe
baking dish lightly with non-stick cooking spray. Place
pears in prepared dish. Combine oats, brown sugar,
flour and spices. Cut in margarine using pastry
blender or 2 knives until mixture is crumbly. Sprinkle
over pears. Cook uncovered on HIGH power 7 to 9
minutes or until pears are tender. Serve warm.

Nutrients per serving:			
Calories	295	Sodium	236 mg
Fat	9 g	Cholesterol	0 mg

Favorite recipe from **The Sugar Association**.

Melon Cooler Salad

Under 200 Calories

Makes 8 servings

1 (8 oz.) pkg. **PHILADELPHIA BRAND®**
    LIGHT Neufchatel Cheese, softened
½ cup frozen lemonade or limeade concentrate,
    thawed
4 cups assorted melon balls

• Place neufchatel cheese and lemonade concentrate
in food processor or blender container; process until
well blended.

• Spoon melon balls into parfait glasses or individual
bowls; top with cream cheese mixture.

Nutrients per serving:			
Calories	140	Sodium	125 mg
Fat	7 g	Cholesterol	25 mg

Melon Cooler Salad

Scalloped Pineapple

Makes 6 servings

1 can (20 ounces) crushed pineapple in pineapple juice
2 tablespoons CRISCO® Shortening
⅛ teaspoon crushed dried mint flakes *or* wintergreen extract
4 bread slices, torn into small pieces
¼ cup milk
2 tablespoons sugar
⅛ teaspoon salt
1 egg, beaten

1. Preheat oven to 375°F. Drain pineapple; reserve juice.

2. Melt Crisco in saucepan; stir in mint. Remove from heat. Stir in pineapple and bread; mix well. Turn into ungreased 1-quart casserole dish.

3. Add milk to reserved juice (you should have 1 cup liquid). Stir in sugar, salt and egg. Pour over pineapple mixture; stir lightly.

4. Bake at 375°F for 40 minutes or until knife inserted in center comes out clean. Serve with whipped topping, if desired.

Nutrients per serving:

Calories	177	Sodium	157 mg
Fat	6 g	Cholesterol	37 mg

5-Minute Apple Crisp

Makes 6 servings

1 (23-ounce) jar MOTT'S® Chunky Apple Sauce
¼ cup margarine
¼ cup firmly packed brown sugar
¼ cup fine dry bread crumbs
¼ cup NABISCO® 100% Bran™
¼ cup chopped walnuts
¼ teaspoon ground cinnamon

Divide apple sauce among 6 greased 6-ounce ovenproof dishes. In medium bowl, blend remaining ingredients and spoon over apple sauce. Broil 4 inches from heat source 5 minutes or until top is golden brown.

Nutrients per serving:

Calories	241	Sodium	124 mg
Fat	10 g	Cholesterol	0 mg

Fruit Sparkles

Makes 6 (½-cup) servings

1 package (4-serving size) JELL-O® Brand Sugar Free Gelatin, any flavor
1 cup boiling water
1 cup cold fruit flavor seltzer, sparkling water, club soda or other sugar free carbonated beverage
1 cup sliced banana and strawberries°
Mint leaves

DISSOLVE gelatin in boiling water. Add beverage. Chill until slightly thickened. Add fruit. Pour into individual dessert dishes. Chill until firm, about 1 hour. Garnish with additional fruit and mint leaves, if desired.

°You may substitute 1 cup drained mandarin orange sections or crushed pineapple for bananas and strawberries.

Nutrients per serving:

Calories	25	Sodium	50 mg
Fat	0 g	Cholesterol	0 mg

Steamed Pears with Raspberry Yogurt Sauce

Makes 4 servings

2 large, fresh California Bartlett pears, pared, halved, cored
Lemon juice
1 package (12 ounces) frozen unsweetened raspberries, thawed
1 teaspoon sugar
¼ cup plain low-fat yogurt

Rub pears with lemon juice to prevent browning. Place pear halves, cut-side down, on steamer rack in large saucepan over boiling water. Cover tightly and steam pears 4 to 5 minutes or until tender when pierced with tip of knife. Cool to room temperature; refrigerate until chilled. Purée raspberries in blender or food processor; strain through sieve to remove seeds. Stir sugar into yogurt. Pour about ¼ cup raspberry purée on each of 4 dessert plates. Place chilled pear half cut-side down in middle of plate on sauce. Spoon about 1 tablespoon yogurt sauce around pear. Garnish with orange zest and mint, if desired.

Nutrients per serving:

Calories	148	Sodium	11 mg
Fat	0 g	Cholesterol	0 mg

Favorite recipe from **California Tree Fruit Agreement.**

Fruit Sparkles

Apple Cinnamon Dessert

Under 200 Calories

Makes 2 servings

1 cup pared diced apple
2 teaspoons REALEMON® Lemon Juice from
    Concentrate
1½ tablespoons sugar
⅛ teaspoon ground cinnamon
2 slices BORDEN® Lite-line® American Flavor
    Cheese Product°, cut into small pieces
½ tablespoon low-calorie margarine
2 plain melba rounds, crushed

Preheat oven to 350°. In small bowl, combine apples,
ReaLemon® brand, sugar and cinnamon; mix well.
Stir in cheese product. Divide mixture between 2
small baking dishes. Top with margarine; sprinkle with
melba crumbs. Bake 12 to 15 minutes or until apples
are tender. Refrigerate leftovers.

°"½ the calories" - 8% milkfat version

Nutrients per serving:			
Calories	123	Sodium	315 mg
Fat	4 g	Cholesterol	5 mg

Apple Cinnamon Dessert

Cherry Cake Cobbler

Low Cholesterol

Makes 16 servings

1 package DUNCAN HINES® Moist Deluxe
    French Vanilla Cake Mix
3 eggs
1⅓ cups water
⅓ cup PURITAN® Oil
1 cup sugar
2 tablespoons cornstarch
2 cans (16 ounces *each*) pitted red tart cherries,
    undrained
2 tablespoons margarine or butter, melted
8 to 12 drops red food coloring
¾ teaspoon almond extract
    Whipped topping or ice cream (optional)

1. Preheat oven to 350°F. Grease and flour 13×9×2-
inch pan.

2. Combine cake mix, eggs, water and oil in large
bowl. Beat at medium speed with electric mixer for
2 minutes. Pour into pan.

3. Combine sugar and cornstarch in large bowl. Add
cherries, melted margarine, food coloring and almond
extract. Stir until blended. Spoon mixture evenly over
batter. Bake at 350°F for 60 to 65 minutes or until
golden. Serve warm or cold with whipped topping or
ice cream, if desired.

Nutrients per serving:			
Calories	269	Sodium	245 mg
Fat	10 g	Cholesterol	40 mg

Spirited Fruit

Under 100 Calories

Makes about 3 cups

¼ cup orange-flavored liqueur *or* orange juice
3 tablespoons REALEMON® Lemon Juice from
    Concentrate
2 tablespoons sugar
3 cups assorted cut-up fresh fruit

In medium bowl, combine liqueur, ReaLemon® brand
and sugar; stir until sugar dissolves. Stir in fruit.
Cover; refrigerate 4 hours or overnight, stirring
occasionally. Serve with cheesecake, pound cake, ice
cream or sherbet. Refrigerate leftovers.

Nutrients per ¼ cup serving:			
Calories	47	Sodium	1 mg
Fat	0 g	Cholesterol	0 mg

Nectarine Creme Fraiche

Under 100 Calories

Makes 4 servings

2 fresh California nectarines, sliced
1 cup plain low-fat yogurt
1 teaspoon honey or sugar
  Few drops almond extract
1 envelope unflavored gelatin
2 tablespoons cold water

Purée nectarines, yogurt, honey and almond extract in blender. Sprinkle gelatin over water in small saucepan. Let stand 1 minute to soften. Stir over low heat until dissolved. Add to nectarine mixture in blender. Blend 10 seconds. Chill until mixture begins to thicken. Spoon into stemmed glasses and chill until set. Garnish with additional nectarine slices and mint sprigs, if desired.

Nutrients per serving:			
Calories	79	Sodium	42 mg
Fat	1 g	Cholesterol	3 mg

Favorite recipe from **California Tree Fruit Agreement**.

Fruit Trifle

Low Cholesterol

Makes 10 servings

1 (10-inch) angel food cake
1 DOLE® Fresh Pineapple
3 firm, medium DOLE® Bananas, peeled,
    divided
3 cups assorted DOLE® fresh fruit
1 pint DOLE® Strawberry or Raspberry Sorbet
2 DOLE® Kiwifruit, peeled, sliced for garnish
1 pint DOLE® Fresh Raspberries for garnish
1 cup DOLE® Pine-Orange-Guava Juice

• Cut cake in half. Freeze one-half for another use. Tear remaining cake into chunks.

• Twist crown from pineapple. Cut in half lengthwise. Cut fruit from shell with a knife. Trim off core and cut fruit into chunks.

• Combine pineapple, 2 of the bananas, sliced and 3 cups assorted fruit in large bowl.

• In 3-quart glass bowl, layer half of the mixed fruit, cake and sorbet. Repeat layers. Top with kiwifruit, raspberries and remaining banana, sliced. Pour juice over all. Cover and refrigerate 1 hour or overnight.

Nutrients per serving:			
Calories	240	Sodium	54 mg
Fat	1 g	Cholesterol	0 mg

Grilled Bosc Pear with Walnuts in Apricot Yogurt Sauce

Grilled Bosc Pears with Walnuts in Apricot Yogurt Sauce

Under 200 Calories

Makes 6 servings

1 orange
1½ cups apricot nectar
½ cup California Walnuts
1½ teaspoons honey
¾ cup plain non-fat yogurt
3 USA ripe Bosc Pears
1 tablespoon California Walnuts, finely chopped

Remove orange peel using vegetable peeler. Cut peel into thin strips 1½ inches in length. Place peel and ½ cup of the apricot nectar in small saucepan over medium-low heat and simmer, stirring often, until nectar has evaporated. Set aside.

In food processor or blender, purée ½ cup walnuts with honey and 2 tablespoons of orange juice squeezed from the peeled orange. Set aside.

In mixing bowl, combine yogurt with remaining 1 cup apricot nectar. Halve and core pears. Leaving skins on, cut pears into thin slices so that slices remain attached to stem end. Fan out pear halves and brush lightly with yogurt mixture. Place pear fans, core-side down, in non-stick skillet. Sear pears over high heat until edges are slightly charred. Set aside.

Place ¼ cup apricot-yogurt mixture evenly onto center of each of 6 serving plates. Spoon 1 tablespoon orange-walnut mixture on one side. Arrange pears on top of walnut mixture. Sprinkle with finely chopped walnuts and reserved orange peel. Garnish with red leaf lettuce, if desired.

Nutrients per serving:			
Calories	181	Sodium	26 mg
Fat	7 g	Cholesterol	1 mg

Favorite recipe from **Walnut Marketing Board**.

Sautéed Bananas

Under 200 Calories

Makes 4 servings

2 tablespoons CRISCO® Shortening
2 tablespoons orange juice
4 firm, ripe bananas
2 tablespoons confectioners' sugar

1. Melt Crisco in large heavy skillet over medium heat. Stir in orange juice.

2. Peel bananas. Cut in half crosswise, then cut each in half lengthwise. Place in skillet and cook over medium heat for 5 minutes, turning once.

3. Arrange bananas in serving dish. Sprinkle with confectioners' sugar. Serve hot.

Nutrients per serving:

Calories	174	Sodium	1 mg
Fat	6 g	Cholesterol	0 mg

Apple-Cheese Snack

Under 100 Calories

Makes 6 (½-cup) servings

1 package (4-serving size) JELL-O® Brand Sugar Free Gelatin, Orange Flavor
¾ cup boiling water
¼ teaspoon ground ginger (optional)
½ cup cold water
  Ice cubes
⅓ cup lowfat cottage cheese
1 small apple, cored and diced

DISSOLVE gelatin in boiling water; stir in ginger. Combine cold water and ice cubes to make 1¼ cups. Add to gelatin, stirring until slightly thickened. Remove any unmelted ice. Measure ¾ cup gelatin; pour into blender. Add cottage cheese; cover. Blend until smooth, about 1 minute. Chill about 15 minutes.

STIR apple into remaining gelatin. Spoon into individual dessert glasses. Chill about 10 minutes. Spoon creamy mixture over fruited gelatin. Chill until set, about 30 minutes.

Nutrients per serving:

Calories	25	Sodium	85 mg
Fat	0 g	Cholesterol	0 mg

Rice Crepes

Under 200 Calories

Makes 10 crepes

1 carton (8 ounces) egg substitute°
⅔ cup evaporated skim milk
1 tablespoon margarine, melted
½ cup all-purpose flour
1 tablespoon sugar
1 cup cooked rice
  Vegetable cooking spray
2½ cups fresh fruit (strawberries, raspberries, blueberries, or other favorite fruit)
  Low-sugar fruit spread (optional)
  Light sour cream (optional)
1 tablespoon confectioner's sugar

Combine egg substitute, milk, and margarine in small bowl. Stir in flour and sugar until smooth and well blended. Stir in rice; let stand 5 minutes. Heat 8-inch nonstick skillet or crepe pan; coat with cooking spray. Spoon ¼ cup batter into pan. Lift pan off heat; quickly tilt pan in rotating motion so that bottom of pan is completely covered with batter. Place pan back on heat and continue cooking until surface is dry, about 45 seconds. Turn crepe over and cook 15 to 20 seconds; set aside. Continue with remaining crepe batter. Place waxed paper between crepes. Spread each crepe with your favorite filling: strawberries, raspberries, blueberries, fruit spread, or sour cream. Roll up and sprinkle with confectioner's sugar for garnish.

°*Substitute 8 egg whites or 4 eggs for 1 carton (8 ounces) egg substitute, if desired.*

Nutrients per crepe:

Calories	111	Sodium	152 mg
Fat	2 g	Cholesterol	1 mg

Favorite recipe from **USA Rice Council.**

Rice Crepes

Meringue Fruit Cup with Custard Sauce

Meringue Fruit Cups with Custard Sauce

Low Sodium

Makes 8 servings

4 large egg whites, at room temperature
½ teaspoon cream of tartar
  Pinch salt
1 cup sugar
1 can (17 ounces) DEL MONTE® Fruit Cocktail, drained
  Custard Sauce (recipe follows)

Line baking sheet with parchment or waxed paper. With bottom of glass, trace eight 3-inch circles about 2 inches apart on paper. Turn paper over on baking sheet. Beat egg whites until frothy; add cream of tartar and salt. Beat until soft peaks form. Add sugar, 1 tablespoon at a time, and beat until meringue is stiff and shiny, about 10 minutes. Transfer to pastry bag fitted with star tip. Use a little meringue to secure paper to baking sheet. Pipe 2 tablespoons meringue in center of each circle; spread to edges. Pipe 2 rings, one on top of the other, around edges of circles. Bake in preheated 200°F oven about 1½ hours or until dry but still white. Cool completely. (Can be made several days ahead and stored in airtight container.)

Spoon fruit into meringue cups. Place on individual dessert dishes. Spoon approximately ¼ cup Custard Sauce over each. Garnish with mint, if desired.

Custard Sauce

4 egg yolks,° slightly beaten
¼ cup sugar
  Pinch salt
2 cups milk, scalded
1 teaspoon vanilla extract

In top of double boiler, mix egg yolks, sugar and salt until well blended. Slowly add milk, stirring constantly. Cook over hot water, stirring constantly, until mixture begins to thicken. Remove from heat; stir in vanilla. Chill. *Makes about 2½ cups.*

°*Use only clean, uncracked eggs.*

Nutrients per serving:			
Calories	217	Sodium	63 mg
Fat	5 g	Cholesterol	115 mg

Apple Baked Pudding

Under 200 Calories

Makes 8 servings

1 cup KELLOGG'S® COMMON SENSE™ Oat Bran cereal, any variety
½ cup sugar
½ cup all-purpose flour
1 tablespoon baking powder
1 teaspoon apple pie spice
2 cups shredded, cored red cooking apples, about 2 medium
3 egg whites
1 teaspoon vanilla
¼ cup sliced almonds

1. Lightly coat 9-inch glass pie plate with vegetable spray; set aside.

2. In large mixing bowl, combine Kellogg's® Common Sense™ Oat Bran cereal, sugar, flour, baking powder and spice. Add apples, stirring to coat.

3. Stir egg whites and vanilla into cereal mixture, mixing until evenly combined. Spread mixture evenly in prepared pie plate. Sprinkle with almonds.

4. Bake in 325°F oven about 30 minutes or until lightly browned. Serve warm.

Microwave Directions: Prepare as above. Cook on HIGH 4 minutes or until top is no longer wet and loses shiny appearance. Let stand 5 minutes before serving.

Nutrients per serving:			
Calories	150	Sodium	147 mg
Fat	2 g	Cholesterol	0 mg

Grape Angel Dessert

Makes 12 servings

¼ cup orange-flavored liqueur
1 tablespoon corn syrup
1 teaspoon grated orange peel
2 cups California seedless grapes
  Custard Sauce (recipe follows)
1 prepared angel food cake (10 ounces), sliced

Bring liqueur and corn syrup to boil in saucepan; add orange peel. Remove from heat; add grapes and marinate 1 hour. To serve, spoon Custard Sauce over each slice of cake and top with marinated grapes.

Custard Sauce: Cream ¼ cup softened butter or margarine and 1¼ cups powdered sugar in saucepan; add 2 tablespoons orange-flavored liqueur and 2 well-beaten egg yolks. Stir in ¼ cup half-and-half; cook over low heat until thickened. Beat 2 egg whites until soft peaks form; beat in egg yolk mixture. Serve warm or chilled. Cover and refrigerate until ready to serve.

Note: *Use only clean, uncracked eggs for Custard Sauce.*

Nutrients per serving:			
Calories	276	Sodium	130 mg
Fat	6 g	Cholesterol	57 mg

Favorite recipe from **California Table Grape Commission**.

Nectarine Macedoine with Ice Milk

Makes 4 servings

2 lemons
½ cup orange juice
½ cup sugar
3 fresh California nectarines, cut into wedges
  (3 cups)
2 cups vanilla ice milk

Squeeze lemons to measure ¼ cup juice. Combine lemon and orange juices, sugar and squeezed lemon shells in small saucepan. Bring to a boil and cook 5 minutes. Remove lemon shells. Pour syrup over nectarines in large bowl. Chill. Top each serving with ½ cup ice milk.

Nutrients per serving:			
Calories	255	Sodium	53 mg
Fat	3 g	Cholesterol	13 mg

Favorite recipe from **California Tree Fruit Agreement**.

Fresh Fruit Parfait

Makes 6 (½-cup) servings

½ cup blueberries
½ cup sliced strawberries
1 package (4-serving size) JELL-O® Brand Sugar
  Free Gelatin, any flavor
¾ cup boiling water
½ cup cold water
  Ice cubes
¾ cup thawed COOL WHIP® Whipped Topping
  Mint leaves (optional)

DIVIDE fruit among 6 parfait glasses. Dissolve gelatin in boiling water. Combine cold water and ice cubes to make 1¼ cups. Add to gelatin, stirring until slightly thickened. Remove any unmelted ice. Measure ¾ cup gelatin; pour over fruit in glasses. Chill until set but not firm.

FOLD whipped topping into remaining gelatin. Spoon into glasses. Chill until set, about 1 hour. Garnish with additional fruit and mint leaves, if desired.

Nutrients per serving:			
Calories	40	Sodium	35 mg
Fat	2 g	Cholesterol	0 mg

Fresh Fruit Parfait

Lemon Ginger Sauce

Exciting

EXTRAS

Lemon Ginger Sauce

Under 100 Calories

Makes ½ cup

½ cup MIRACLE WHIP® FREE Nonfat
    Dressing
2 tablespoons lemon juice
1½ tablespoons packed brown sugar
1 teaspoon *each* grated lemon peel, ground
    ginger

• Mix together ingredients until well blended;
refrigerate. Serve over fresh fruit.

Nutrients per serving (2 tablespoons):			
Calories	60	Sodium	370 mg
Fat	1 g	Cholesterol	0 mg

Fruit Spreads

Under 200 Calories

Makes about 2 cups (10 servings)

2 cups fresh berries
1½ cups sugar

Wash, drain and crush berries. In medium saucepan,
combine berries and sugar. Cook over medium heat
until sugar is dissolved, stirring constantly. Increase
heat and bring to a rapid boil, again stirring
constantly. Cook about 10 minutes or until jam is
thick and small amount dropped onto a saucer stays in
place. Cool completely. Fruit spreads should be
stored in tightly sealed container in refrigerator and
will keep about 4 weeks.

Note: Recipe can be made with blackberries,
blueberries, raspberries or strawberries.

Nutrients per serving:			
Calories	117	Sodium	1 mg
Fat	0 g	Cholesterol	0 mg

Favorite recipe from **The Sugar Association.**

Fruited Yogurt Shake

Under 100 Calories

Makes 9 (½-cup) servings

3 cups cold lowfat milk
1 package (4-serving size) JELL-O® Sugar Free
    Instant Pudding and Pie Filling, any flavor
1 container (8 ounces) plain lowfat yogurt
1 cup crushed ice
1 medium banana, cut into chunks°

COMBINE all ingredients in blender in order given;
cover. Blend at high speed 1 minute. Pour into
glasses. Serve immediately.

°*You may substitute ½ cup sliced strawberries for
banana chunks.*

Nutrients per serving:			
Calories	90	Sodium	210 mg
Fat	2 g	Cholesterol	10 mg

Banana Pineapple Colada

Under 200 Calories

Makes 2 servings

½ ripe banana
½ cup fresh or canned pineapple
½ cup pineapple juice
½ cup ice cubes
1 tablespoon sugar
¼ teaspoon coconut extract

Combine all ingredients in blender or food processor;
process until smooth. Pour and serve immediately.

Nutrients per serving:			
Calories	198	Sodium	5 mg
Fat	0 g	Cholesterol	0 mg

Favorite recipe from **The Sugar Association.**

Quick and Creamy Cocoa Dip for Fruit

Quick and Creamy Cocoa Dip for Fruit

Under 200 Calories

Makes 4 servings

1 carton (8 ounces) low-fat vanilla or honey
   yogurt
1 tablespoon unsweetened cocoa powder
4 fresh California peaches, plums, nectarines or
   Bartlett pears (or any combination), sliced

Combine yogurt and cocoa in serving bowl. Serve
with sliced fruit.

Tip: To keep fruit colors bright and prevent browning,
dip sliced fruit in mixture of 1 tablespoon lemon juice
and 1 cup water.

Nutrients per serving:			
Calories	116	Sodium	38 mg
Fat	2 g	Cholesterol	0 mg

Favorite recipe from **California Tree Fruit Agreement.**

Iced French Roast

Under 100 Calories

Makes 2 servings

2 cups brewed French roast coffee, strong
2 tablespoons low-fat milk
2 teaspoons sugar
½ teaspoon cocoa powder
   Dash ground cinnamon

Combine all ingredients in blender; blend until
smooth. Pour over ice and serve immediately. Or
refrigerate to serve later.

Nutrients per serving:			
Calories	27	Sodium	13 mg
Fat	0 g	Cholesterol	1 mg

Favorite recipe from **The Sugar Association.**

Peach Fizz

Makes 6 servings

3 fresh California peaches, sliced
1 can (6 ounces) pineapple juice
¼ cup frozen limeade or lemonade concentrate, undiluted
¼ teaspoon almond extract
Finely crushed ice
3 cups club soda, chilled

Purée peaches in blender or food processor to measure 2 cups purée. Stir in pineapple juice, limeade concentrate and almond extract. Fill six 12-ounce glasses ⅔ full with crushed ice. Add ½ cup peach mixture to each; top with club soda. Stir gently.

Nutrients per serving:			
Calories	65	Sodium	6 mg
Fat	0 g	Cholesterol	0 mg

Favorite recipe from **California Tree Fruit Agreement**.

Low-Calorie Hot Cocoa

Makes four 1-cup servings

⅓ cup NESTLÉ® Cocoa
4 cups skim milk, divided
8 envelopes powdered non-nutritive sweetener
Non-dairy whipped topping and additional NESTLÉ® Cocoa, for garnish
Cinnamon sticks, optional

In 2-quart saucepan, combine cocoa and about ¼ cup of the milk, stirring until smooth paste forms. Gradually whisk in remaining milk. Cook over medium heat, stirring frequently, until bubbles form around edge of pan. Remove from heat; stir in sweetener until dissolved.

Pour into 4 heatproof mugs. Garnish servings with non-dairy whipped topping; sprinkle with cocoa. Serve with cinnamon sticks.

Nutrients per serving:			
Calories	140	Sodium	124 mg
Fat	4 g	Cholesterol	10 mg

Cocoa Cinnamon Topper

Makes 1¼ cups

1 cup QUAKER® Oat Bran hot cereal, uncooked
1 teaspoon grated orange peel (optional)
¼ cup sugar
1 tablespoon unsweetened cocoa
½ teaspoon ground cinnamon

Heat oven to 350°F. Place oat bran in ungreased 13×9-inch baking pan. Bake 15 to 17 minutes or until light golden brown, stirring occasionally. Stir in orange peel; cool. Add sugar, cocoa and cinnamon. Store tightly covered at room temperature. To serve, sprinkle generously on fruit, fruit salads, low fat yogurt, ice milk or pudding. Or use as a topping for muffins by sprinkling on batter just before baking.

Microwave Directions: Place oat bran in 1-qt. microwavable bowl. Microwave at HIGH 2 to 3 minutes, stirring every minute. Stir in orange peel; cool. Proceed as above.

Nutrients per serving (1 tablespoon):			
Calories	25	Sodium	0 mg
Fat	0 g	Cholesterol	0 mg

Cocoa Cinnamon Topper

Apple Butter

Makes about 1 pint (32 servings)

1 pound cooking apples
½ cup water
½ cup packed brown sugar
¼ teaspoon ground cinnamon
Dash *each* ground cloves and allspice

Wash, remove stems and quarter apples. Place apples and water in large saucepan and cook slowly until soft. Squeeze fruit through a fine strainer to yield 1 cup apple pulp. Add brown sugar, cinnamon, cloves and allspice. Cook over low heat, stirring frequently, until sugar is dissolved. Continue cooking and stirring until mixture is thick and brown and no liquid separates around edge of butter when a small amount is spooned onto a saucer.

Note: For larger amounts (more than 1 pound of apples), measure apple pulp and add ½ cup packed brown sugar for each cup of apple pulp.

Nutrients per 1 tablespoon serving:

Calories	21	Sodium	1 mg
Fat	0 g	Cholesterol	0 mg

Favorite recipe from **The Sugar Association.**

Nectarine Punch Cooler

Makes 6 servings

1 pint fresh strawberries, hulled and rinsed
2 medium fresh California nectarines, cut into wedges
1 can (6 ounces) frozen pineapple or cranberry juice concentrate, undiluted
12 ice cubes, cracked
1 to 2 cups sparkling water, chilled

Reserve 6 whole strawberries for garnish. Purée remaining strawberries, nectarines and frozen juice concentrate in blender. Add ice and blend until smooth. Pour into punch bowl or large container. Stir in sparkling water. Serve with reserved strawberries and additional nectarine slices, if desired.

Nutrients per ½ cup serving:

Calories	87	Sodium	4 mg
Fat	0 g	Cholesterol	0 mg

Favorite recipe from **California Tree Fruit Agreement.**

Apricot Frappé

Makes 6 servings

2 cups apricot nectar
½ cup PHILADELPHIA BRAND® LIGHT Pasteurized Process Cream Cheese Product
1 cup diet ginger ale
3 tablespoons orange juice or orange flavored liqueur
½ teaspoon vanilla
3 ice cubes

- Gradually add nectar to cream cheese product in food processor or blender container; process until blended.

- Add ginger ale, orange juice and vanilla; process until well blended. Add ice; process 1 minute. Serve in chilled glasses. Garnish with fresh fruit, if desired.

Nutrients per serving:

Calories	100	Sodium	120 mg
Fat	3 g	Cholesterol	10 mg

Strawberry Frosty

Makes 6 servings

1 (8 oz.) container PHILADELPHIA BRAND® Soft Cream Cheese with Strawberries
1 pt. strawberries, hulled
1 cup frozen strawberry lowfat yogurt
1 cup diet lemon-lime carbonated beverage
1 tablespoon sugar or 3 packets sugar substitute

- Place cream cheese and strawberries in food processor or blender container; process until blended.

- Add frozen yogurt, carbonated beverage and sugar; process until well blended. Serve over ice, if desired.

Nutrients per serving:

Calories	190	Sodium	115 mg
Fat	10 g	Cholesterol	35 mg

Apricot Frappé and Strawberry Frosty

Pear Berry Crush

Under 100 Calories

Makes 2 servings

1 package (10 ounces) unsweetened frozen
    raspberries or strawberries
1 fresh California Bartlett pear, cored, coarsely
    chopped
12 ice cubes, cracked

Combine all ingredients in blender; blend until
smooth.

Nutrients per serving:			
Calories	97	Sodium	3 mg
Fat	0 g	Cholesterol	0 mg

Favorite recipe from California Tree Fruit Agreement.

Orange Sunriser

Low Sodium

Makes 4 servings

1 can (6 ounces) frozen orange juice concentrate
2 cups low-fat (1%) milk
¼ cup sugar
3 tablespoons instant malted milk powder
1 teaspoon vanilla extract
10 ice cubes, crushed

Combine all ingredients in blender; process until
smooth.

Nutrients per serving:			
Calories	211	Sodium	62 mg
Fat	3 g	Cholesterol	10 mg

Favorite recipe from The Sugar Association.

Banana-Date Shake

Banana-Date Shake

Low Cholesterol

Makes 2 servings

2 ripe, medium DOLE® Bananas, peeled
1 DOLE® Orange, peeled
1½ cups DOLE® Pure & Light Orchard Peach
    Juice, chilled
¼ cup DOLE® Dates
    Cracked ice, optional

Place all ingredients in blender except cracked ice.
Process until smooth. Add cracked ice while blending
for frosty cold shake.

Nutrients per serving:			
Calories	205	Sodium	14 mg
Fat	1 g	Cholesterol	0 mg

Cranberry Cool

Under 200 Calories

Makes 4 servings

2 cups low calorie cranberry apple drink
½ cup PHILADELPHIA BRAND® LIGHT
    Pasteurized Process Cream Cheese Product
1 cup frozen vanilla lowfat yogurt

• Gradually add cranberry apple drink to cream
cheese product in food processor or blender
container; process until blended.

• Add frozen yogurt; process until well blended. Serve
over ice, if desired.

Nutrients per serving:			
Calories	150	Sodium	170 mg
Fat	5 g	Cholesterol	15 mg

Acknowledgments

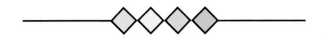

*The publishers would like to thank the companies and organizations
listed below for the use of their recipes in this book.*

Almond Board of California
Best Foods, a division of CPC International Inc.
Borden Kitchens, Borden, Inc.
California Apricot Advisory Board
California Table Grape Commission
California Tree Fruit Agreement
Carnation, Nestlé Food Company
Checkerboard Kitchens, Ralston Purina Company
Chilean Winter Fruit Association
The Dannon Company, Inc.
Del Monte Corporation
Dole Food Company
Hershey Chocolate U.S.A.
Keebler Company

Kellogg Company
Knox Gelatine, Inc.
Kraft General Foods, Inc.
Libby's, Nestlé Food Company
Mott's U.S.A., a division of Cadbury Beverages, Inc.
Nabisco Foods Company
Nestlé Chocolate and Confection Company
New York Cherry Growers Association, Inc.
Ocean Spray Cranberries, Inc.
The Procter & Gamble Company, Inc.
The Quaker Oats Company
The Sugar Association
USA Rice Council
The Walnut Marketing Board

Photo Credits

*The publishers would like to thank the companies and organizations
listed below for the use of their photographs in this book.*

Best Foods, a division of CPC International Inc.
Borden Kitchens, Borden, Inc.
California Apricot Advisory Board
California Tree Fruit Agreement
Chilean Winter Fruit Association
The Dannon Company, Inc.
Del Monte Corporation
Dole Food Company
Knox Gelatine, Inc.

Kraft General Foods, Inc.
Libby's, Nestlé Food Company
Mott's U.S.A., a division of Cadbury Beverages, Inc.
Nabisco Foods Company
Nestlé Chocolate and Confection Company
The Procter & Gamble Company, Inc.
USA Rice Council
The Walnut Marketing Board

Index